TerryGami

Animals, Birds, and Gnomes
By

Terry Cleveland Crowley

By Terry Cleveland Crowley
Cover and Logo Design by Terry Cleveland Crowley
Copyright © 2011, All Rights Reserved.
First Edition, First Printing
ISBN: 987-0-9836513-1-4
Scribe Craft Publishing
www.terrygami.com

Special Thanks

I will be eternally grateful to my critter vetting crew for all of the time and candor they have lent to this project: Liz Jameson, Lucy Turner, Anita Davis, Cathy Ballard, Linda Guy, Mary Ann Chlopan, and the Wirgau and friends. Special thanks to Liz Jameson for lending her editing expertise to the project. Thanks, too, to my sons, Sean and Brendan, for their much needed technical support throughout the years. Without them, I would still be fiddling with computer programs or in despair over a computer crash. A special thanks to my mother, Rose Cleveland, for encouraging me to press on through the years. Thank you to all of my Tallahassee Writers Association friends and acquaintances for their guidance and suggestions. Also, big thank you to Elaine Partnow, Donna Meredith and Sharon McFall for their invaluable input.

I am sure more suggestions will come from the crafters, both young and old, as this craft evolves. And, again, a special thanks to the Boo Boo Bunny creator whomever and wherever he or she may be. Fortunately, my attempt to remember how to make the Boo Boo Bunny 24 years ago ended up looking more like an owl or a baby chick, and so began the craft I have named TerryGami – for the terrycloth from which the creatures are made.

With Much Thanks to All!

TCC
December 2011

Please Read:
The materials recommended in the instructions for TerryGami critters and holiday icons involve the use of small decorative pieces for the facial features, safe, non-toxic, non-flammable fabric glue, scissors, rubber bands or string, and needle and thread. The use of these materials should be supervised by an adult, especially when used by young children or anyone who does not possess sufficient maturity. When hanging an ornament on a tree, take care not to put it directly onto a light, just as one would do for any ornament. Be sure to use non-flammable, non-toxic glue. Also, be sure to take extra precautions when babies, toddlers, and pets are present.

Table of Contents

Introduction 5

General Instructions and Tips 7

Party Tips 11

Sewing by Hand on Terrycloth 14

Bear 15

Monkey 24

Tortoise 31

Hare 37

Duck 42

Fish 47

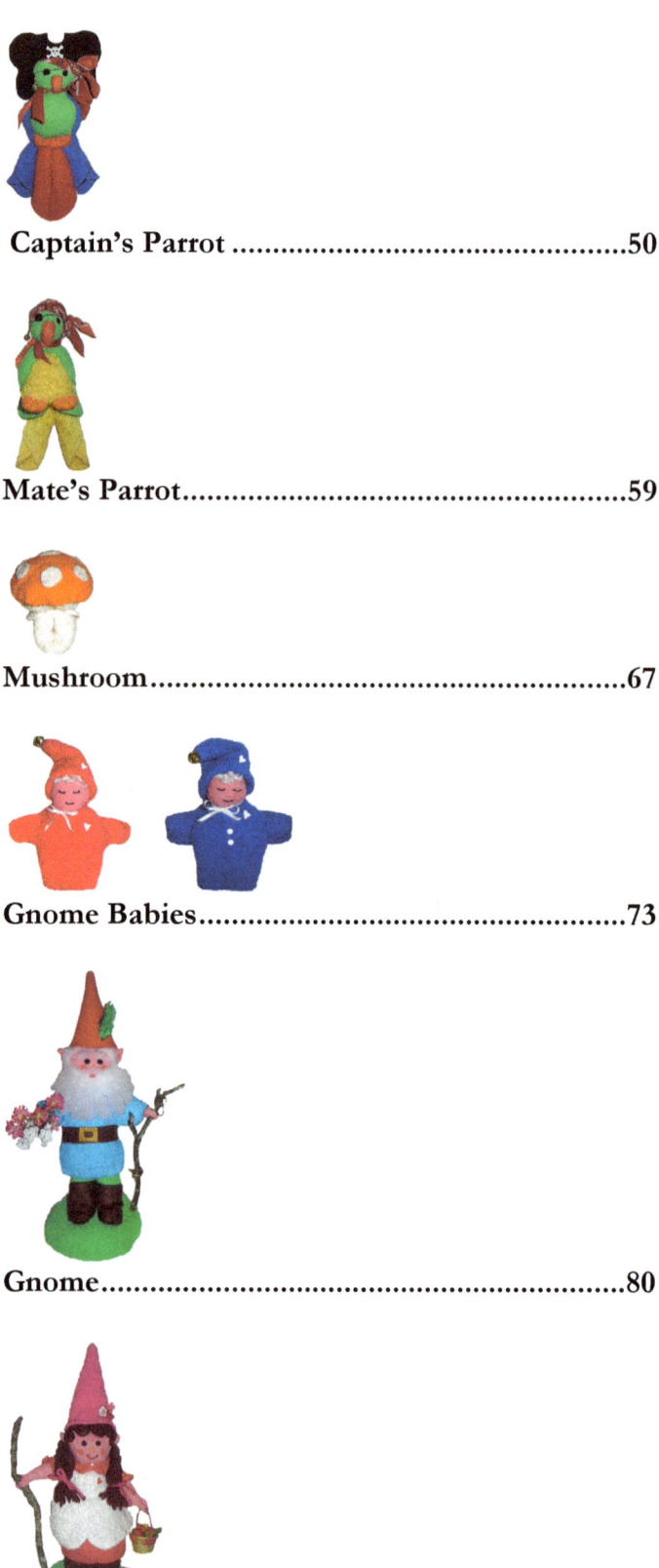

Captain's Parrot 50

Mate's Parrot 59

Mushroom 67

Gnome Babies 73

Gnome 80

Gnome Girl 93

Introduction

What is TerryGami? TerryGami is a new craft that uses thin, borderless terrycloth washcloths or terrycloth utility cloths, rubber bands and glue or needle and thread to make animals and holiday icons. Some of the critters are stuffed, some are not. All of the items can be made with thin washcloths that can be purchased at department stores for about $4 for a package of 18 cloths (2011 prices depending on the store). The critters may require one to four washcloths, depending on the item being made. Several of the items do not require gluing or sewing. For safety, blunt-end needles such as darning and small yarn needles work well with terrycloth. Learning to sew is a necessary life skill, and TerryGami is a fun way to learn it.

Many of the terrycloth creations will be of interest to teachers for use in their classrooms, to parents who home-school, to all kinds of Scout leaders, to Bible school teachers and summer camp leaders, to Boys and Girls Club facilitators, to play group moms and to children who enjoy making crafts on their own. Since the trend now is for children to have craft birthday parties, the party favor or activity can be a terrycloth soft sculpture the children can make themselves, saving parents money in the process. Educators and group facilitators are always looking for hands-on activities for children. These critters will appeal to both girls and boys. Leaders of children's groups of all kinds will now have another solution to that ever-looming question, "What are we going to do for the meeting this week?"

The holiday icons can be used as table decorations, ornaments on a tree or as stuffed toys. The Easter Bunny can easily fill the kids' baskets with a variety rabbits, chicks, and Easter eggs. For Halloween, bats and ghosts can be a fun craft for a party. For Valentine's Day, the heart box can hold a special treat. Party Poppers can be made for a Fourth of July party or any party or holiday, for that matter. In Scotland and England, for instance, Party Poppers are a tradition on New Year's Day.

Parents can use the book as a gift for elementary school teachers, art teachers and Bible school teachers or as a present for children. Materials such as a colorful bundle of washcloths and rubber bands, a package of foam board or glass gems, and needle and thread can be wrapped up with the book. A sewing kit would make a nice companion to go along with the book.

TerryGami offers a chance for children to improve their dexterity and learn how to follow directions. It will help children to develop their fine motor skills because it requires them to shape and mold, roll and glue or sew the project. Once they learn how to make basic body structures, children will be creating critters of their own design.

Parents who are willing to spend time making presents for their child's classmates will find many creative ideas. The end product can be a keepsake to remember a special day, like the Graduation Owl for a kindergarten graduation or the Heart Box for Valentine's Day. If the idea of making 20 critters by yourself does not appeal to you, have a TerryGami sewing bee with some other parents. Crafters and children will be interested in many of the terrycloth creations for church bazaar sales. They are inexpensive and easy to make and can serve multiple purposes.

Imaginative ideas abound for the usage of these versatile creatures:
- The holiday items can be used as ornaments on a tree or as a toy.
- With the addition of a potpourri bag, items can be used as sachets or as a place to tuck a special treat or a trinket.
- Many of the items can be made as gifts for parents such as the heart box for Valentine's Day with a candy Kiss or potpourri bag in it or the Angel as an ornament for a Christmas gift.
- With a strategically placed ice cube, several of the critters can be used on a boo boo, too.
- Since all of the items are made of terrycloth, the holiday icons and other creatures can be used to decorate a bathroom. For example, the turkey can sit on top of a stack of towels.
- TerryGami can help Girl Scouts earn their sewing merit badge or business-wise merit badge, if they make the critters to sell. Boy Scouts require an entrepreneur merit badge. Children can make TerryGami critters to sell at bazaar sales or at a TerryGami stand, instead of a lemonade stand.
- Pediatric occupational therapists can use this craft in their therapy sessions to help children improve their fine motor skills and hand-eye coordination. In fact, occupational therapists for adults may find this craft useful.
- Seniors at senior centers will enjoy learning this new craft for their grandchildren.

Children with the maturity level of roughly 8- years old and up can make these craft items. Adults will need to assist children at first, especially young children. Also the basic critter can be prepared ahead of time for younger children, and then children can add on the facial features and decorations later.

TerryGami critters and holiday icons are a fun way to learn to sew. A critter like the Snowman can be used to teach children how to sew on buttons by using buttons for the eyes as well as down the front of the body. Different types of sewing stitches, like the running stitch or the whip stitch, for example, can be taught. Blunt-end needles can be used with young children or adults. Darning and yarn needles have wide eyes for easy threading, as well as the plastic needles.

TerryGami provides another creative outlet for children and provides a special activity to do with them on a rainy day or during the summer months. In the not-too-distant past, girls and boys alike were enthralled with collectable, small, stuffed animals. Now they will be able to make their own critters, which will give more meaning to their collection because the children will be able to say, "I made this!" Senior centers may also embrace TerryGami, and activity directors will appreciate yet another fun craft that many elders will enjoy.

Textile companies now produce thin washcloths or terrycloth utility cloths in beautiful colors, including colors that lend themselves well to making animals, reptiles and birds. However, children seem to prefer the bright colors over traditional colors for the critters. They choose blue and yellow bears, and purple and pink chicks. Perhaps, one day, a stack of beautiful washcloths will excite children the same way a new box of Crayons and a new tub of Play Doh® excite them now.

TerryGami General Tips

Occasions for Making TerryGami Critters
- TerryGami critters and holiday icons make great projects for home schooling or in the classroom, for Bible school and summer camps, for activities or treat bag favors for birthday and holiday parties, as a play date or sleepover activity, as a craft for Girl Scouts and Boy Scouts and other children clubs such as Indian Guides and Indian Princesses. Just make sure the project fits into your time schedule. For the more time consuming projects, plan them out over a several days, if necessary. Also crafters can use many of these items for bazaar sales and as holiday tree ornaments, as well as stocking stuffers and Easter basket cloth toys.

Safety First - Making Critters for Babies and Small Children
- Always keep sharp tools, small objects and rubber bands away from babies, toddlers, and small children who put things in their mouths. It would be best to wash the cloths first.
- Embroider the facial features and decorations on the critters for infants and toddlers to prevent choking on small items.
- It is best to sew the critter, instead of gluing it, especially for babies, even though many brands of fabric glue are non-toxic and non-flammable.

Washcloths
- Terrycloth washcloths or terrycloth utility cloths can be purchased in bulk at some discount department stores, in a package of 18 for $4. They come in every color imaginable, but don't worry if you can find the appropriate color for a critter, because the children will happily make a pink or yellow tortoise, for example. The cloths labeled "washcloths" are generally a bit softer than the ones labeled "utility cloths." This may be important when choosing cloths for babies.
- While thin terrycloth washcloths are ideal, any 12" by 12" washcloth can be used, especially washcloths without ribbed borders. Granted, some washcloths may be too thick for some designs, and of course, they are much, much more expensive then the ones sold by the bundle in discount department stores. Also, experiment, because the new fabric-like paper napkins may work with some of the patterns. Paper napkins tear easily, but the instructions can be used in some of the designs. A 10" x 10" or an 11" x 11" cloth can be used for most creatures. Of course, the smaller the cloth, the smaller the critter, which may be good when making tree ornaments for any holiday. Sometimes the cloths are 11" x 12", but it won't make

any difference in the project. Experiment with the smaller sizes. The 10" x 10" cloth is ideal for the Easter egg.
- Check for various textures and sizes of cloths in grocery stores, dollar stores and discount department stores.
- Always roll the cloths so that the tag remnant is on the inside of the roll. Otherwise, the remnants of the tag may ruin the appearance if it shows, for example, in the ears of a critter or on the beard of the Santa. Sometimes the tag remnant can be ripped or pulled out of the seam.
- When winding or rolling up a cloth, children may find it helpful to place the first roll up against something like a book or another object, so it won't unwind. When they are finished rolling both sides of the cloth, just turn the rolls face down to prevent them from unwinding.
- Use plastic bag clamps, spring clothespins or extra rubber bands to hold the body parts (like the arms, legs, hats, antlers, etc.) in place while gluing or sewing. Small plastic bag clamps work well on most items, especially when gluing. Extra rubber bands can be very useful, too, for holding items in place, while sewing or gluing. Just cut them off to prevent snags.
- Roll the cloths with the amount of tension recommended in the instructions. If it is not stated how tightly to roll the roll, just roll with a medium tension.
- If in some instructions it is hard to determine which end is which while making the critter, mark it with a safety pin or fabric chalk to help you keep track. For example, it helps to know which end is the beard in the Santa and which end is for the ears in the Sleepy Bunny instructions.
- Experiment with decorative cloths. Just cut the material to the correct size. Material with a little thickness will have better results than material such as thin cotton.
- Don't worry too much about snags in the terrycloth. Just trim any snags.

Rubber Bands
- Use medium-sized rubber bands that can be wrapped at least twice around the cloth.
- Purchase colorful rubber band balls. This makes the experience even more fun for kids.
- If using a rubber band to hold an item in place while sewing or gluing, for example an arm or leg, it may be best to cut the rubber band off, rather than risk getting snags in the material while you are removing it.
- It is sometimes helpful to match the rubber band to the washcloth color. However, please note that in most designs the rubber bands are covered with a ribbon, yarn, jute or material, so it doesn't necessarily matter in most cases.
- Often, the rubber band may be cut from the critter if the area around it has been sewed. For example, the rubber band around the neck can often be cut off once the shoulders are sewn.
- Other types of rubber bands, like orthodontic or dreadlock rubber bands, work well in certain areas where it may be difficult to cover the rubber band, for example, around the ears of the hare.

- While rubber bands are easy to use and expand when you need them to, plain old string and yarn can be used instead of rubber bands when making the critter; just be sure to tie the knot tightly and use a double knot to secure it.

Sewing or Gluing the Critters
- **Glue:** Use clear, quick drying clear fabric glue for the best results when gluing a critter. **Check for toxicity and flammability.** Fabric glue is preferred and there are safe fabric glues available at craft stores. Also, check online for safe glue for use by children, if you cannot find it locally.
- All critters and holiday icons can be sewed instead of glued. Sewing yields a better, softer result. Also, glue often has to dry before you can proceed with the next step.
- **Needles:** Use blunt-end needles such as small yarn or darning needles for young children, especially. The larger yarn needles are okay, but sometimes you have to work to get them through several thicknesses of material. These needles work well for adults, too, because they are easy to thread. Plastic needles work okay, too. Darning needles or small yarn needles are preferable. Terrycloth lends itself well to blunt-end needles because of the wide weave of the cloth. Use regular sewing needles on felt, if making the snowman's hat.
- For the most part, it is best to apply the glue with a toothpick or cotton swab to avoid a mess, in case it comes out of the bottle too quickly. Also, the glue can ruin the looks of a project because it is not that easily removed from terrycloth, especially hot glue, which is impossible to remove. Unless you are very adept at using a hot glue gun, it is not recommended. Hot glue can make unforgivable mistakes.
- Match the thread to the washcloth and the thread will be barely noticeable, if at all. If you want to tear out the seam to redo it, just pull the area to find it because the thread may be hard to find.
- If a child is having difficulty keeping the fabric together as he or she sews, use small bag clips to hold the material together. For example, bag clips will hold the item together while the child sews the seam. They can also be used to hold an area in place while the glue dries. Clothespins and other clips work, too.
- Embroidering facial features is necessary when using the critter as a baby gift to prevent choking (see page 12), or just leave the facial features off all together.

Decorating the Critters
- Experiment with the faces using acrylic or glass gems, beads, sequins, pom-poms, yarn, buttons, sticky-backed foam, felt, wood pieces and Googly Eyes for the features. Paint the wooden pieces with non-toxic craft paint. Sticky-back foam board is the quickest and easiest to use along with a hole-puncher, but you need to use glue to make sure it is permanently attached. Precut pieces of foam board are available in craft stores, such as flowers, hearts, snowflakes, and many other items. Glue these pieces on even though they have a sticky back. The spokes of the snowflakes can be used as eyelashes; just cut them in half. Now, glittered foam board is available for a more festive appearance!

- Crafters may also want to experiment with natural items for the facial features like dried watermelon and pumpkin seeds, dried beans or small pods.
- For a classier sheen, dust the ornaments with white, fairy dust glitter or a fine, white glitter. Do not use a flammable fixative! Most of the glitter should stick without it. Shake it out over a piece of paper to get rid of the excess.

To Hang as an Ornament
- Thread a needle with a single 10-inch strand of gold or silver lamé, or yarn. Do not tie a knot in the end. Sew through the top of the ornament, leaving several inches at the end. Unthread the needle, and then tie a double knot with the two ends to make a loop.
-

Dexterity
- Crafts are often used to improve dexterity. Washcloth crafts should deliver in a big way in this regard because children and adults must roll and shape the cloths, attach them with a rubber band or string, and then sew or glue them together. They also have to prepare the materials for the facial features. Reading and deciphering the instructions requires another skill set, which may be beneficial to handicapped and brain injured individuals.

Extra Tips
- Be sure to measure the ears and antlers, etc. make sure they are even and the same size. Measure the circumference of the arms and legs with a tape measure, especially if you are planning to sell it or give the item as a gift.
- If you sew instead of glue the item, you can always redo it easily, if necessary, because the thread can be easily ripped out. Be sure to trim snags with scissors and remove lint and other debris that clings to the terrycloth.
- If the rubber band shows at a certain point on the critter, use the excess material around the area to cover it, and then tack it down by sewing or gluing it.
- When sewing, you will have a problem with the knot at the end of your thread going right through the cloth. See the "Sewing by Hand" chart under Sewing on Terrycloth (page 12).
- Note: Always use the whip stitch when sewing the critters. Use the running stitch for sewing the hat or other items made of felt.
- To make as a sachet: Fill a small cloth bag with potpourri, and then find a place on the item to tuck it inside of the critter. For example, tuck it inside of the baby chick's stomach or the heart box, and sew it up. It can then be used as a sachet for a dresser drawer.

Degree of Difficulty
- The fish, duck, hare, mushroom, and baby gnomes don't require much sewing or gluing. The other animals are medium range in difficulty because the arms, legs, and bodies all require sewing. The adult gnomes require a lot of sewing, so allow enough time to complete them. Start with the easier items!

TerryGami Party Tips

In a TerryGami birthday or holiday party (or group activity), the critter or holiday icon is both the party activity and the party favor! Not only is this activity fun for the children, they learn a new life skill – how to sew. With a little preparation, the party will run smoothly.

Pick one project, and then make it yourself several days or even a week before the party. This will help you when you demonstrate the project to the children. Use the completed project as the center piece for the table so the children will be able to compare and refer to it as they work. Difficult projects may take an hour or more to make, especially if you have a large group of children, so one project will probably be plenty.

By preparing for the party in advance, you will be able to round up the materials and determine what supplies to ask the children to bring, like rulers and safe blunt-end scissors, but do have a few extra on hand in case someone forgets to bring them. Each child should have his or her own to use. You will want to provide the blunt-end yarn or darning needles to avoid needle pricks. Blunt-end needles are ideal when working with children because they are very easy to thread due to the wide eye of the needle. Terrycloth lends itself well to using these needles because of the loose weave of the material.

TerryGami Birthday Party

Some of the more labor intensive projects will require time, so it may help to ask a few parents or grandparents to join the party to help you trouble shoot. If no one is available, teach your child so he or she can help the others in a pinch. Keep an eye out for those who are quick studies and ask them to help the others, too. Children will need help threading the needle and tying a knot in the thread for the first time. Also, demonstrate how to keep the knot from going through the terrycloth (see the Hand Sewing chart). Demonstrate a few simple slip stitches when they are ready to sew, and be sure to show them how to tie off the thread once they are finished sewing. Kids are tickled to learn how to sew and they are very proud of their own creations.

The girls learn to sew at a TerryGami birthday party.

Go over the general instructions and materials list, keeping in mind that you may already have some of the craft items in the house, like foam board and ribbon. Provide each child with a plastic cup with his or her name on it. This will help them keep their items together, such a needles, pre-cut ribbon, facial features, rubber bands and glass gems.

Children seem to want to use a variety of colorful washcloths or terrycloth utility cloths, especially for the animals. They may prefer to make a purple or yellow bear, instead of a brown one, and a pink or blue chick, instead of a yellow one. So if the appropriate color isn't available, don't worry; just provide a variety of colorful cloths. Children also love to stuff the critters, so don't be surprised if they go overboard on the quilt batting. Quilt batting is recommended because it can be easily cut into strips for stuffing the arms and legs. Most cloth bundles have three cloths of each color, which is perfect for most projects. Many projects only require one or two cloths.

Checklist of possible supplies you will need:

Rulers
Scissors
Clear small cups for each child to put their small materials
Yarn or darning needles (blunt-end needles) and regular needles, if using felt for the hat
Matching thread for all of the washcloth colors, check dollar stores for small spools of thread

Ribbon, yarn, or jute, twine, gold or silver cord or lamé
Medium sized rubber bands, matching the material, if possible, but not necessary
Clear fabric glue, non-toxic, non-flammable
Toothpicks or cotton swabs for applying the glue
Hole punchers for foam board or boo boo cards (heart, star, round and square shapes)
Terrycloth washcloths or utility cloths
Felt squares
Foam board or foam board cutouts, sequins, glass or acrylic gems
Tracing paper or thin typing paper for tracing patterns, if necessary
Pencil
Bag clips to hold parts of the project while sewing (optional)
Quilt batting
Tulle
Potpourri and measuring cup
Card stock or heavy paper to make boo boo cards
Refreshments and paper plates, napkins, cups, forks and spoons
Tablecloth or table covering

Proud of their pink, purple, yellow, blue and orange turtles/tortoises and hares!

Schedule a mini snack break during the party, if craft time is running long. A drink and some cookies or fruit will make it festive. Do this away from the craft project to avoid spills and mishaps. Parents will find they enjoy the party, too, as they see how their children's creative spirit is fostered.

Sewing by Hand

Tie a knot at the end of the thread.

Always double the thread. First, moisten the index finger. Grasp the double strand of thread about two inches from the bottom. Wrap the end around the index finger, allowing the very end to overlap about 1/2 inch. With the thumb and index finger, roll the threads together, and then off of the finger. Pull the knot tight with the thumb and finger. Note: There are videos online that demonstrate this.

Sewing on Terrycloth

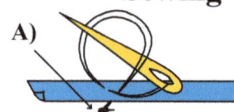 

When sewing on terrycloth material, **A)** tie a big knot in the end of the thread and pull the needle through the fabric gently so the knot will not come out. Now go back in again with the needle near the same spot. As you bring the needle up again, make a loop in the thread and bring it through the loop. This will anchor he knot so it will not pull through the material as you sew. **B)** If it doesn't matter if the knot shows, bring the needle through the material, but leave the knot above the material and bring the needle through the two strands of thread to anchor the thread. Blunt-end needles such as darning and yarn needles work well with children and adults because they are much easier to thread, given the wide eye of the needle.

Sewing on Buttons

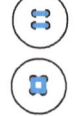  

To sew on a button: Thread the needle and double the thread. Tie a knot in the end of the thread. Pull the needle through the material and one of the holes at the bottom of the button, and then pull the thread though. Choose one of the patterns above, making several passes through each hole until the button is secure. To use on the face of a critter: Just catch the material in the spot where you want it. It may help to mark the spot where you want the button. Make sure the knot does not show. Use a regular needle.

Whip Stitch

Use this stitch!

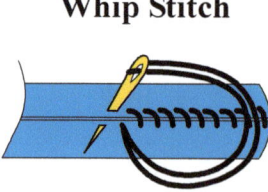

Bring the edges of the cloth together, and then pull the needle through the fabic on each side, keeping the stitches about a quarter of an inch apart. This is the stitch to use when sewing the seams of the TerryGami critters.

Running Stitch

Use this stitch on felt items.

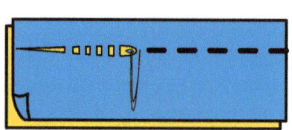

Use the running stitch for mending and gathering material. Draw the needle through the material several times, and then pull the thread through. Repeat the process. Use this to make hats and shoes. Also, you will need to use a regular needle for the felt pieces.

Tying-Off the Stitches

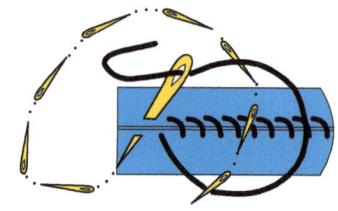

When you come to the end, make a loop with the thread, and then bring the needle through the loop several times. Repeat this method one or two times to make sure it is secure.

Embroidery

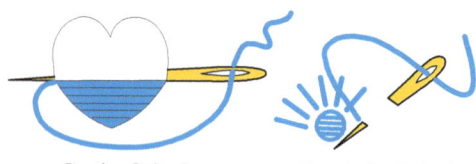

Satin Stitch   **Straight Stitch**

Note: Unauthorized circulation of these instructions is prohibited and is a violation of copyright. Items made for sale from these instructions must say on the hang tag and/or in the description on a website: "This is an original design by T. C. Crowley from her TerryGami books."

Bear Factoids

- Bears are mammals that have a large body with stocky legs, shaggy hair, a long snout and a short tail.
- They are classified as caniforms which means they are doglike and carnivorous.
- Like dogs, bears have a keen sense of smell.
- Most bears are omnivores, but the Panda bear eats plants and the polar bear eats mostly meat.
- Bears can climb trees, can swim and are fast runners. Bears mark their territory by biting, clawing and rubbing trees.
- Bears live in burrows and caves during the winter months, sleeping for long periods of time.
- Bears can weigh 600 pounds and can measure up to 6'5" tall.
- Morris Michtom was inspired to make a stuffed toy bear and to call it a "Teddy" bear because U.S. President Teddy Roosevelt refused to shoot a bear the members of his hunting party had clubbed and tied to a tree.

TerryGami Bear Instructions

Materials:
*Three thin, tan terrycloth washcloths, approximately 12" x12"
*Black and red glass gems or sparkle foam board for eyes, heart nose, and heart
*Clear fabric craft glue (non-toxic and non-flammable)
*One 1/4" or 1/2" wide ribbon, 12" long
*Three medium rubber bands, plus extra, if gluing
*Quilt batting
*Needle and matching thread (blunt-end needle optional)
*Hole puncher 1/4" for eyes (optional)
*Heart hole puncher 1/4" for the nose and heart (optional)
*Black tatting thread 3/4 inch
*Scissors
*Ruler

Finished size: Approximately 7"w x 6"t.

1. Cut the tags off the cloths. Place two cloths flat on a flat surface in a diamond shape. Roll the opposite corners to the center of each cloth. One cloth will be a part of the body and the other one will be the legs. Turn the cloths over so they won't unroll.

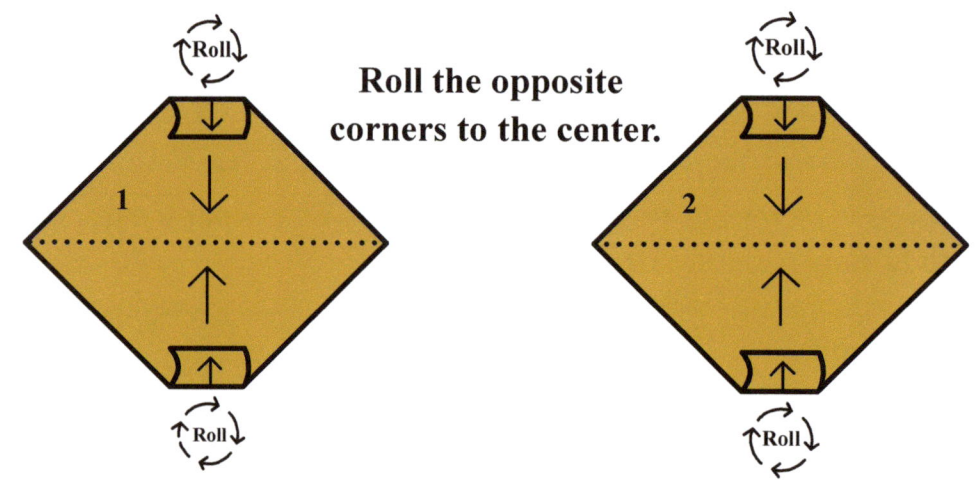

The washcloths will look like this.

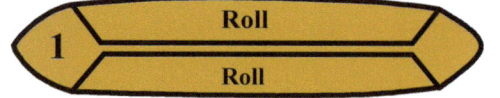
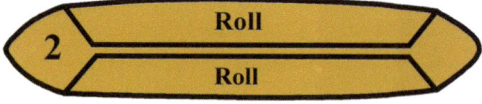

This cloth will be half of the body. **This cloth will be the legs.**

Continue...

TerryGami Bear Instructions

2. **A)** Place the third cloth on a flat surface in a diamond shape. **B)** Fold the top and bottom corners so that the corners meet in the center. **C)** Turn the cloth over, holding the corners in place. Pin or lightly tape in place, if necessary. **D)** Roll the folded sides to the center. The corners will flip up. **E)** The cloth will look like this. This cloth will be part of the body. The center corners will become the ears. Turn the cloth over so it doesn't unroll.

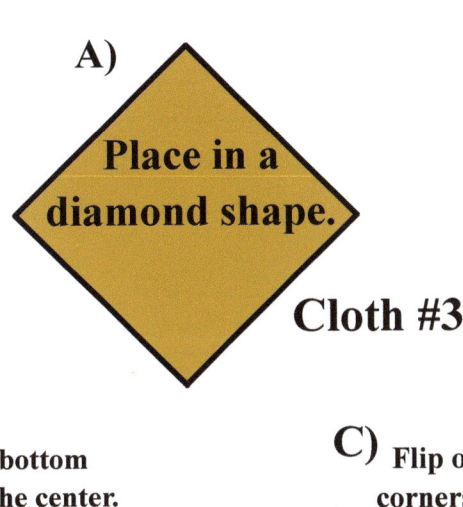

B) Fold the top and bottom corners to meet in the center.

C) Flip over with corners in place.

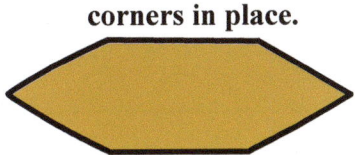

D) Roll the sides to the center.

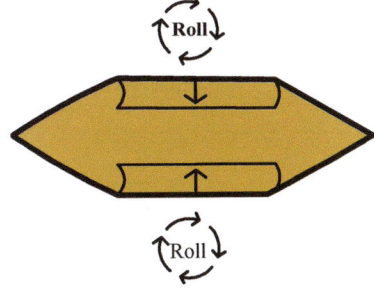

E) This is what the cloth will look like.

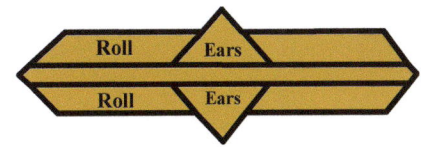

This piece is part of the body.

Continue...

TerryGami Bear Instructions

3. Stack cloths one and three. The third cloth (ear cloth) should be on the bottom with the rolls facing down and the first cloth should be on top with the rolls facing up.

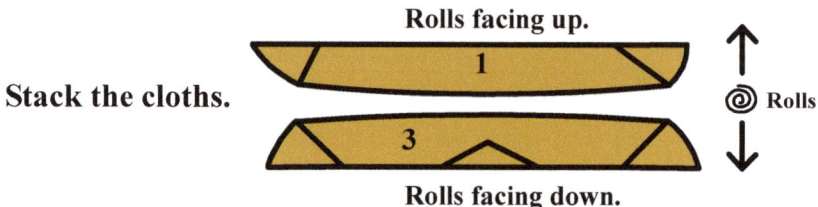

---

4. Measure down four inches from the corners on the left end, and then wrap a rubber band. Measure down 5 inches from the corners on the other end, and then wrap a rubber band. The 5-inch end will be the arms. The 4-inch end will remain tucked inside of the body.

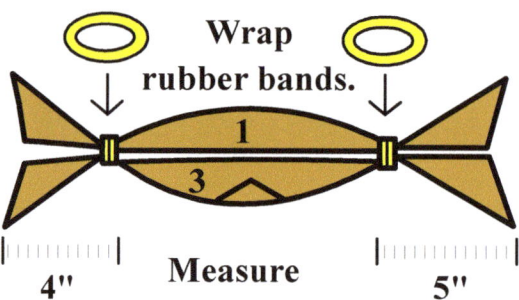

---

5. Now turn the ensemble inside out so that all of the corners are on the inside, including the corners that will become the ears.

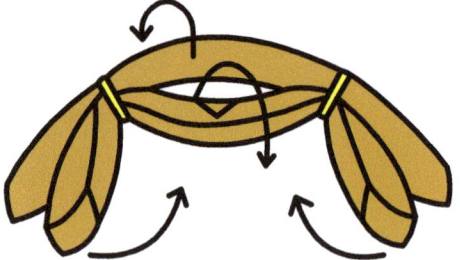
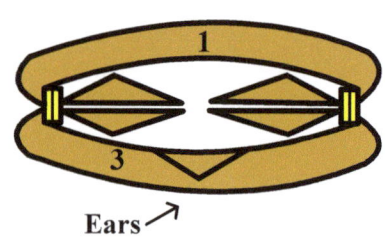

Continue...

18

TerryGami Bear Instructions

6. **A)** Turn the ensemble upright, and then **B)** pull out the top 5-inch corners, one on each side. They will be the forelegs. The bottom corners remain tucked inside of the body.

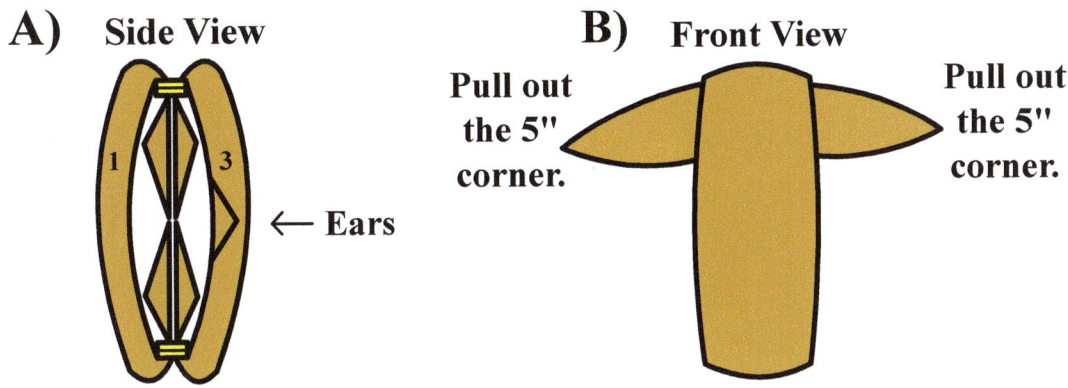

7. **To form the head and ears: A)** Roll the side with the ears up above the rubber band. **B)** Measure down 2 inches from the top. Wrap a rubber band at this point, making sure the ears are above the rubber band.

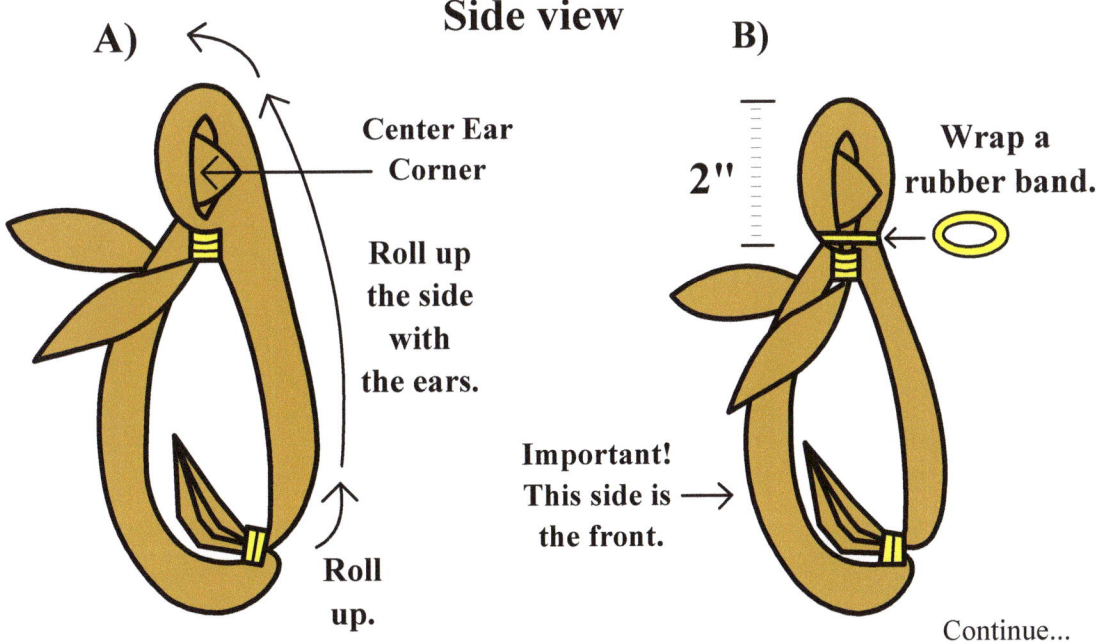

Continue...

19

TerryGami Bear Instructions

8. **For the body and head:** Separate the rolls slightly inside of the head and stomach, leaving the bottom corners tucked inside. Add stuffing to the head and the stomach.

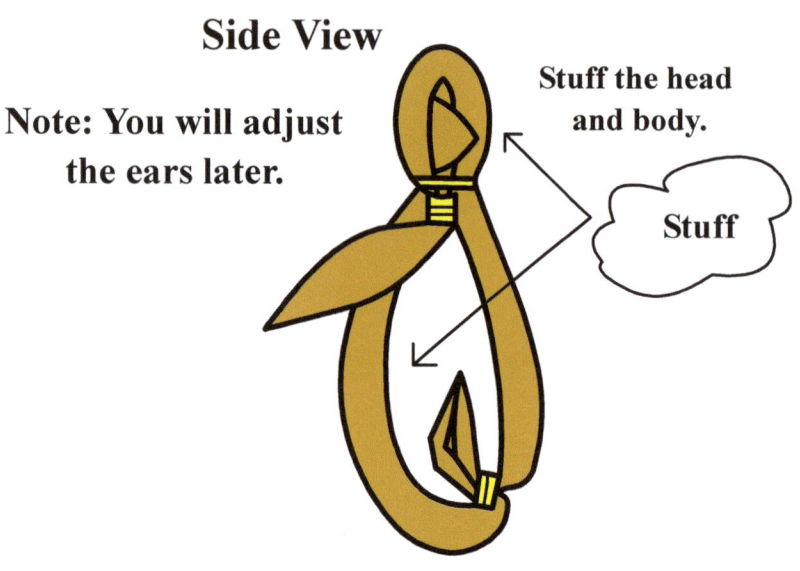

---

9. **To form the legs:** Pull #2 cloth through the bottom of the body, making sure the legs are even and that the rolls are facing down.

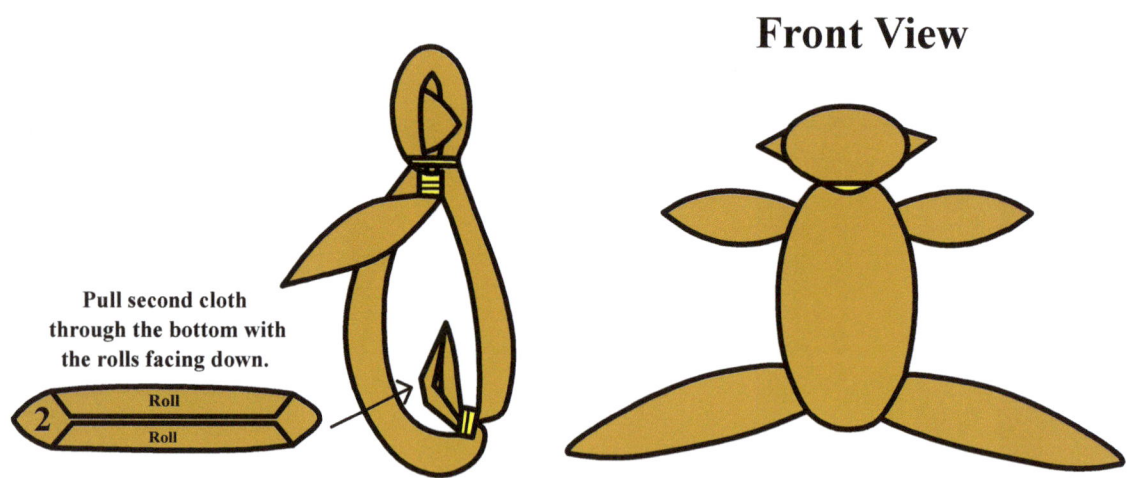

Continue...

TerryGami Bear Instructions

10. **For the arms and legs:** Fold the tip of the corner under on a leg until it measures 2 inches for the fore leg or arms and 2 1/2 inches for the hind legs. Roll the limbs, one side to the center, and then the other side to the center. (See the diaram in the box.) Add stuffing to the limbs. Sew or glue the seams together. Twist the arms and legs so the seams face downward. Sew or glue the hind legs into a sitting position. Sew or glue the front and back shoulders together.

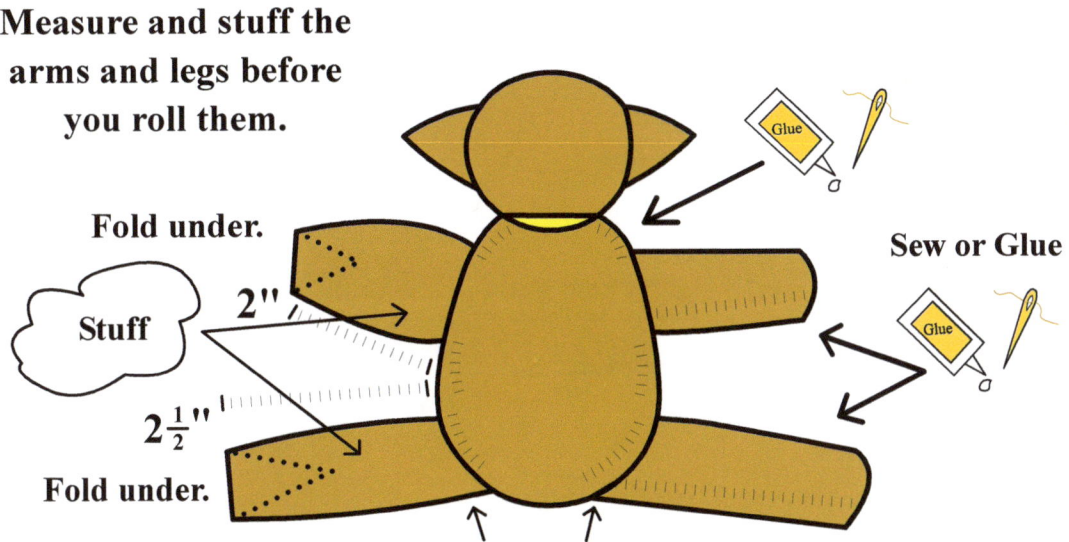

Measure and stuff the arms and legs before you roll them.

Fold under.

Stuff 2"

2½"

Fold under.

Sew or Glue

Sew or glue the legs forward.

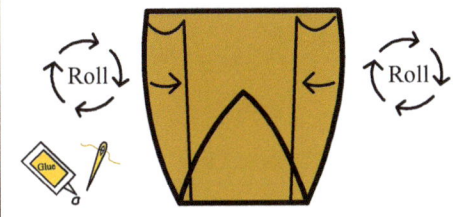

Underside view of the arms and legs.

Fold the tip of the corner under, and then roll each side to the center. Sew or glue seams together.

Continue...

TerryGami Bear Instructions

11. Pull the ears up on top of the head and round and shape them. Tuck the excess material into the head. Sew or glue the sides of the head, and then sew or glue the ears to the top of the head. Sew or glue the sides of the body closed. Sew or glue above the arms to cover the rubber bands.

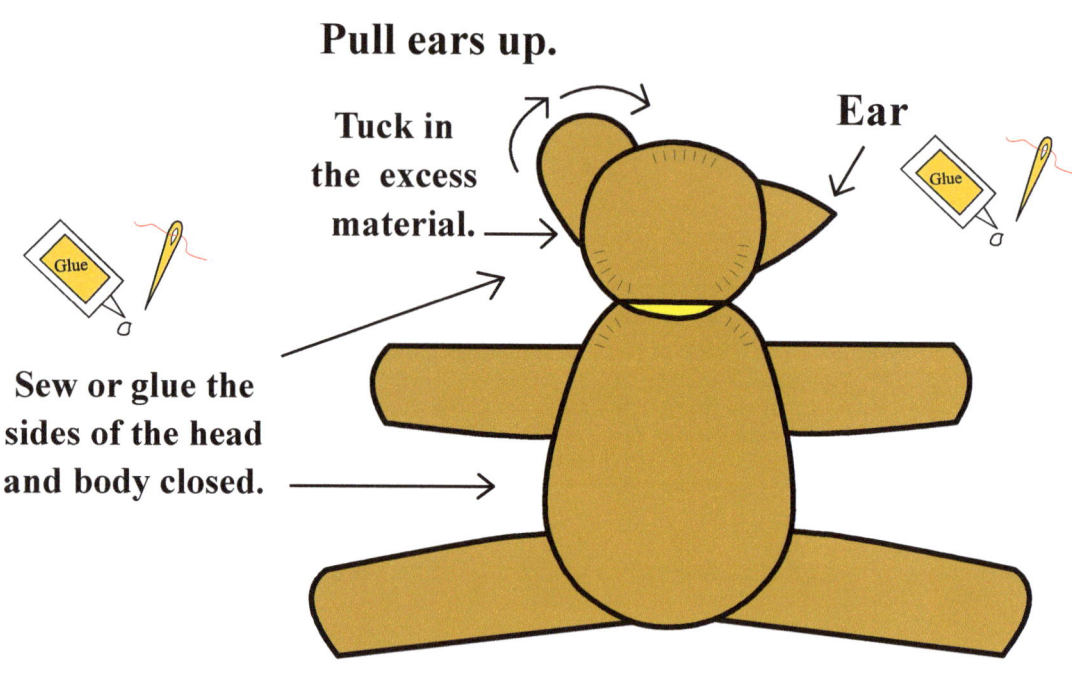

12. Prepare the facial features. Make a pattern and cut out, or use hole punches, or other materials like glass gems.

Patterns:

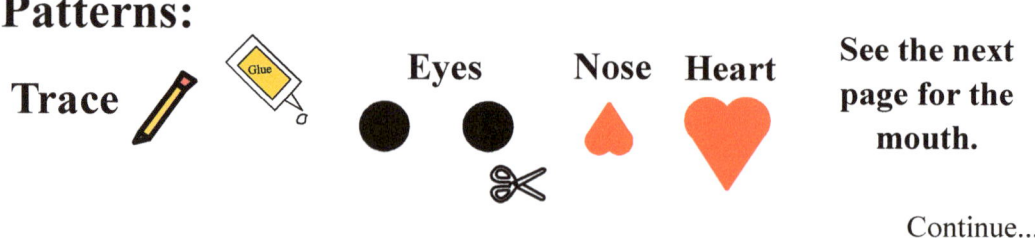

Continue...

TerryGami Bear Instructions

13. Glue on the eyes, nose and heart. Cut one 12-inch piece of ribbon, and then tie bow around the neck. **For a mouth**: Cut one 1/2-inch and one 1/4-inch piece of tatting thread, and then glue it on to the face (optional). Trim the thread to fit.

Mouth

14. Trim any snags in the material. Suggestion: Make the bear from red washcloths for St. Valentine's Day. Use clear heart gems for for the nose and heart. Use a white bow around the neck.

Warning: Keep small objects, sharp items and rubber bands away from small children.

Monkey Factoids

- Monkeys are primates. Primates are any order of mammals that have hands and/or feet for grasping, binocular vision, a large brain and a shortened snout.
- Monkeys live in trees or on the ground, and eat leaves, seeds, fruit, nuts, flowers, eggs, small insects and small animals.
- The smallest monkey, the pygmy marmoset, is only 5 or 6 inches long.
- The largest money is the mandrill, which is over 3 feet long and weighs 77 pounds.
- Most monkeys have prehensile tails, and the ones without tails are sometimes called apes, such as the Barbary macaque.

TerryGami Monkey Instructions

Materials
* Three thin, brown terrycloth washcloths approximately 12" x 12"
* Two thin, cream terrycloth washcloth approximately 12" x 12"
* Three medium rubber bands
* Four pieces of yarn (2 cream and 2 black) each 15 inches long
* Small piece of black foam board for eyes and nose
* Clear fabric glue (non-toxic and non-flammable)
* Needle and matching thread
* Tatting thread 1 1/2"
* Quilt batting
* Hole punches 1/4" and 1/8" (or for the 1/8" nose, just cut two tiny pieces)
* Scissors
* Ruler

Finished size: Approximately 10"w x 12"l.

1. Cut the tags off of all of the cloths, and then place them on a flat surface in a diamond shape. Roll the opposite corners to the center of the cloths.

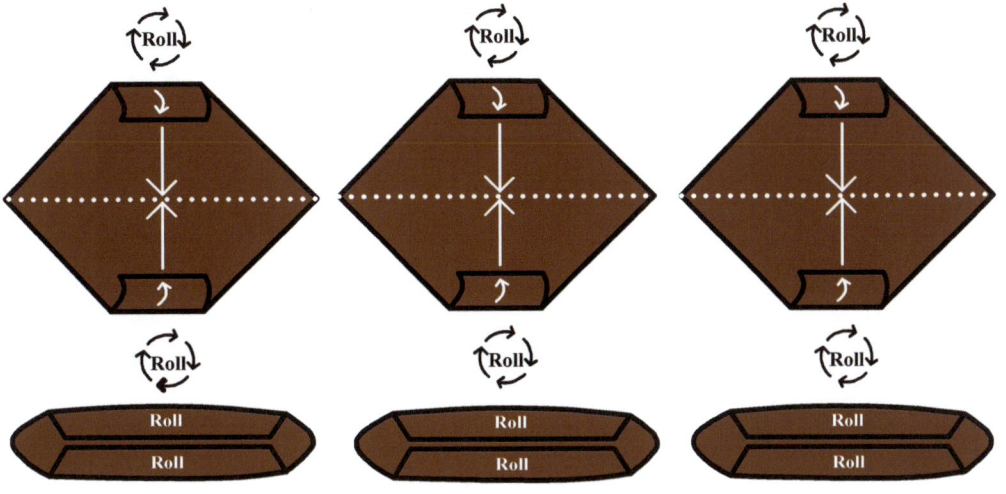

They will look like this.

2. Stack two cloths with the rolls on the bottom cloth facing down and the rolls of the top cloth facing up. Measure down 5 inches on one end, and then wrap a rubber band. Measure down 3 inches on the other end, and then wrap a rubber band.

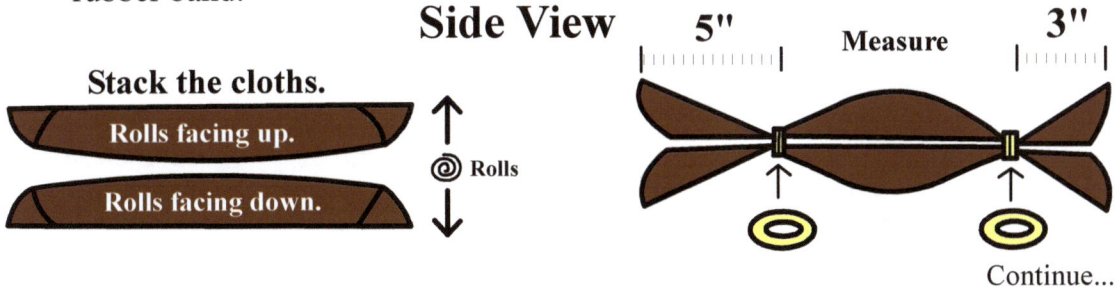

Continue...

25

TerryGami Monkey Instructions

3. Open the hole between the cloths.

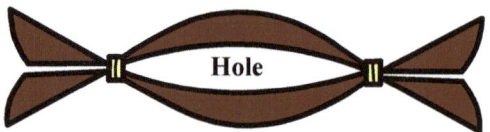

A side view showing the rolls facing the outside.

---

4. Turn the cloths inside out so that the rolls are now facing each other on the inside, and the corners are on the inside, too.

Turn the cloths inside out.

The rolls and corners will now be on the inside.

---

5. Turn the cloths upright with the longer corners on the top. Roll one side up to form the head, and then measure down 2 inches from the top. Wrap a rubber band at this point.

The longer corners on the inside are the arms of the monkey.

Side View

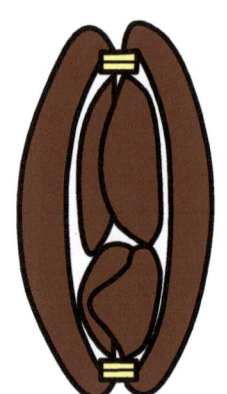
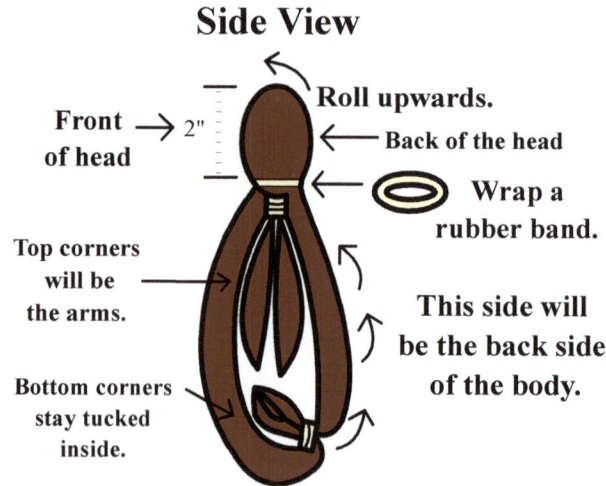

Top corners will be the arms.

Bottom corners stay tucked inside.

Front of head → 2"

Roll upwards.
Back of the head
Wrap a rubber band.
This side will be the back side of the body.

Continue...

26

TerryGami Monkey Instructions

6. Pull the top corners out, one on each side. Pull the third brown cloth through the bottom of the body, making sure the bottom corners of the legs are even. Turn the rolls to face the bottom so they do not show. Spread out the rolls (partially) inside of the head and stomach. Stuff them with batting, filling the area in between the rolls.

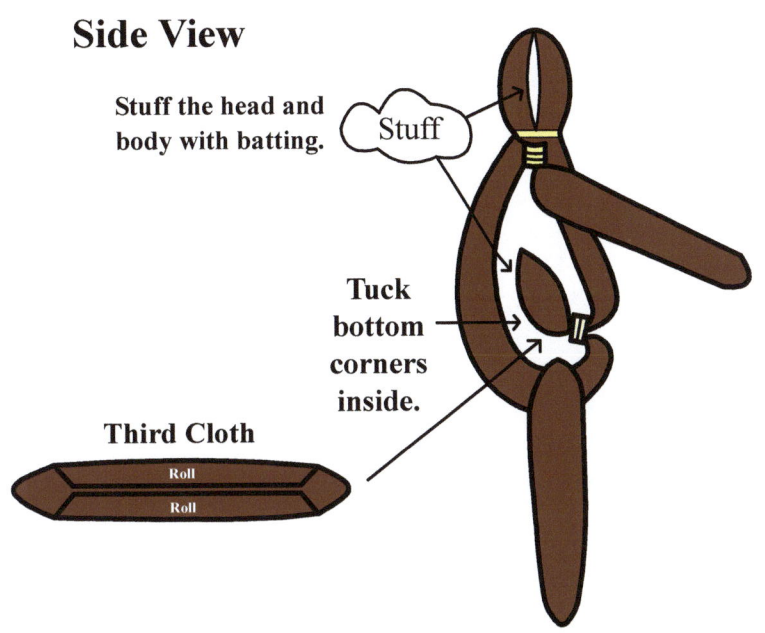

7. **A)** Measure down 3 inches on two corners of the cream cloths to make the ears. **B)** Cut off the excess on each end of the corners (an inch or so on each end), and **C)** stack the two pieces together and sew or glue the two pieces together.

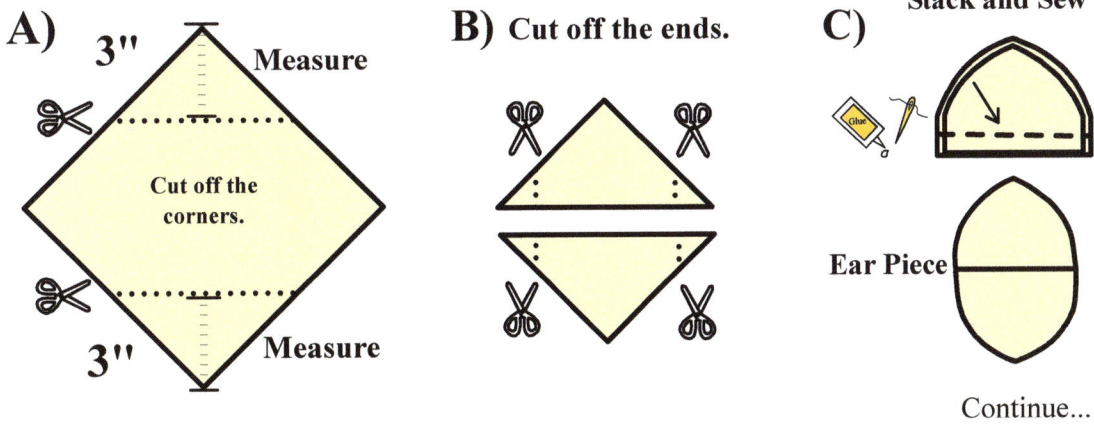

Continue...

TerryGami Monkey Instructions

8. **A)** Turn the ear piece so the seam runs vertically. **B)** Pull the ear piece through the hole in the side of the head. **C)** Shape the ears to the desired size and shape, and then sew or glue the sides of the head closed.

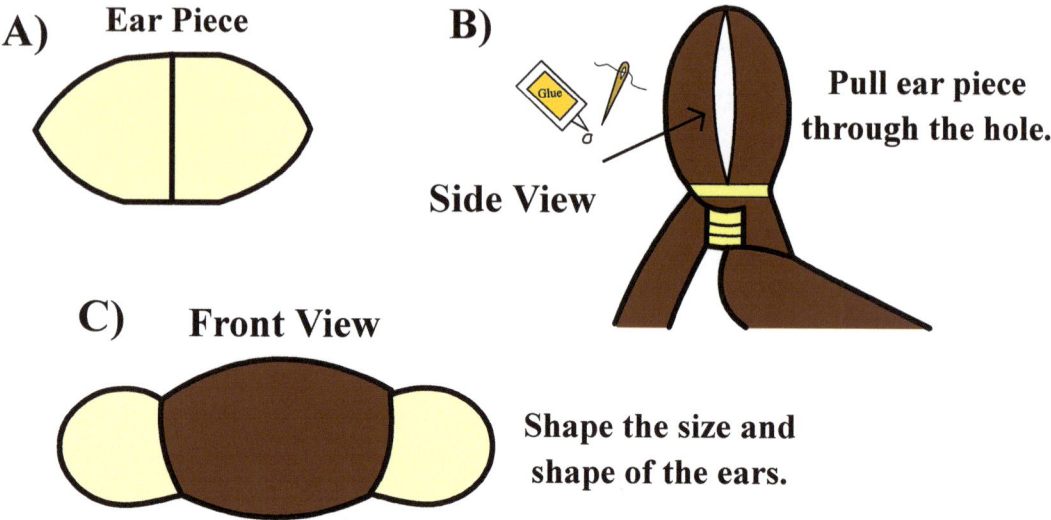

9. Re-roll the arms and legs, stuff them, and then sew the seams closed, leaving about 2 1/2 inches open on each end of the arms and legs so you can add the cream cloth for the hands and feet. (See the next page.)

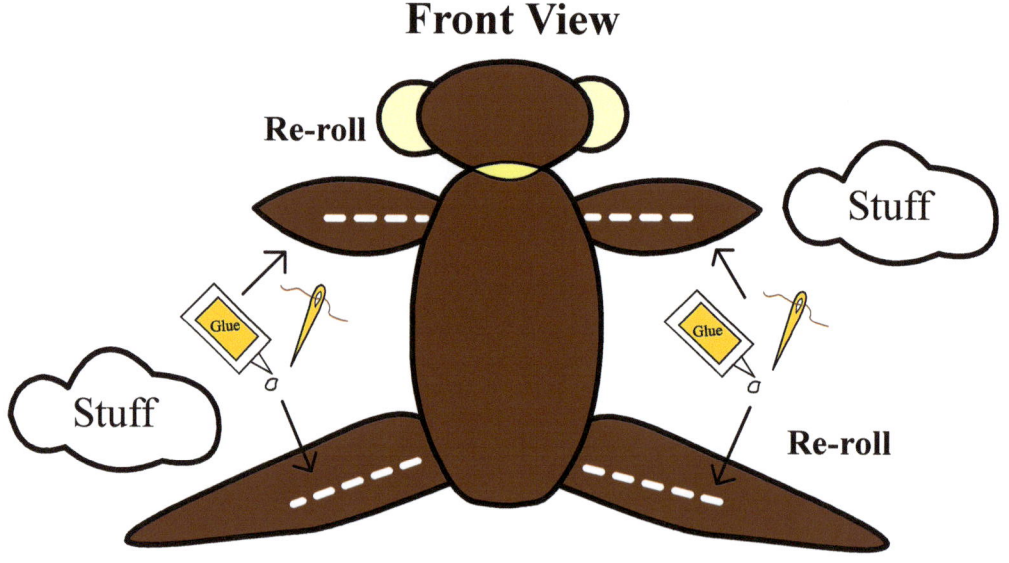

Continue...

TerryGami Monkey Instructions

10. **A)** Cut four 2" x 4" rectangles out of the cream cloth to make the hands and feet. **B)** Fold the pieces in half and sew up the edges on two sides. **C)** Turn inside out, and then add a little batting to the end.

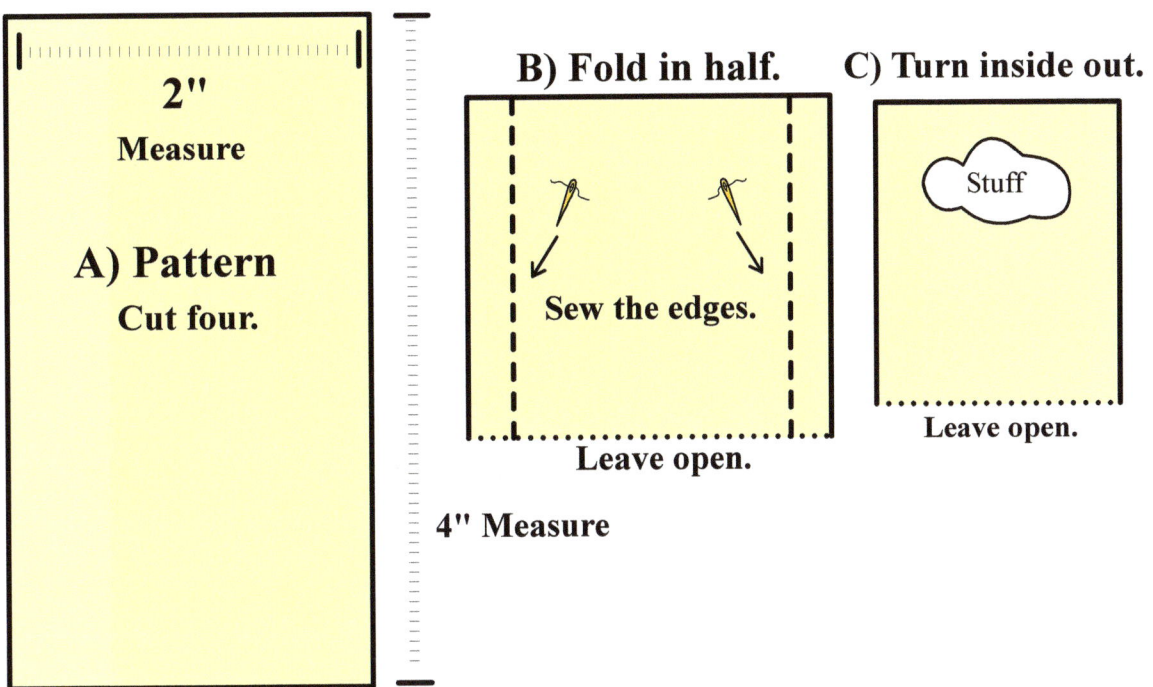

11. Put the feet and hand pieces inside of the opening of arms and legs. Re-roll the arms and legs around the the cream pieces. Sew or glue them closed. Sew or glue around the edges of the hands and feet to make sure they are secure. Glue on the face piece.

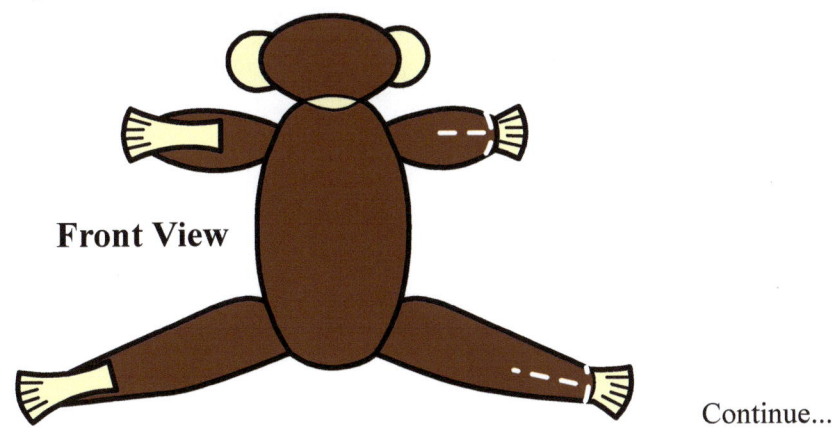

Continue...

TerryGami Monkey Instructions

12. Trace and cut out the patterns for the face. Trace and cut out the patterns for the eyes and nose, or use large and small hole punch. Cut about 1 1/2 inches of tatting thread or yarn for the mouth, and trim to fit. Glue on the facial features. The heart is optional. Trim any snags in the material.

Patterns:
Trace

Eyes **Nose** **Mouth**

$1\frac{1}{2}"$ Measure

Note: Tiny hole punches are hard to find. Cut triangles instead, if necessary.

Monkey Face
Cut One

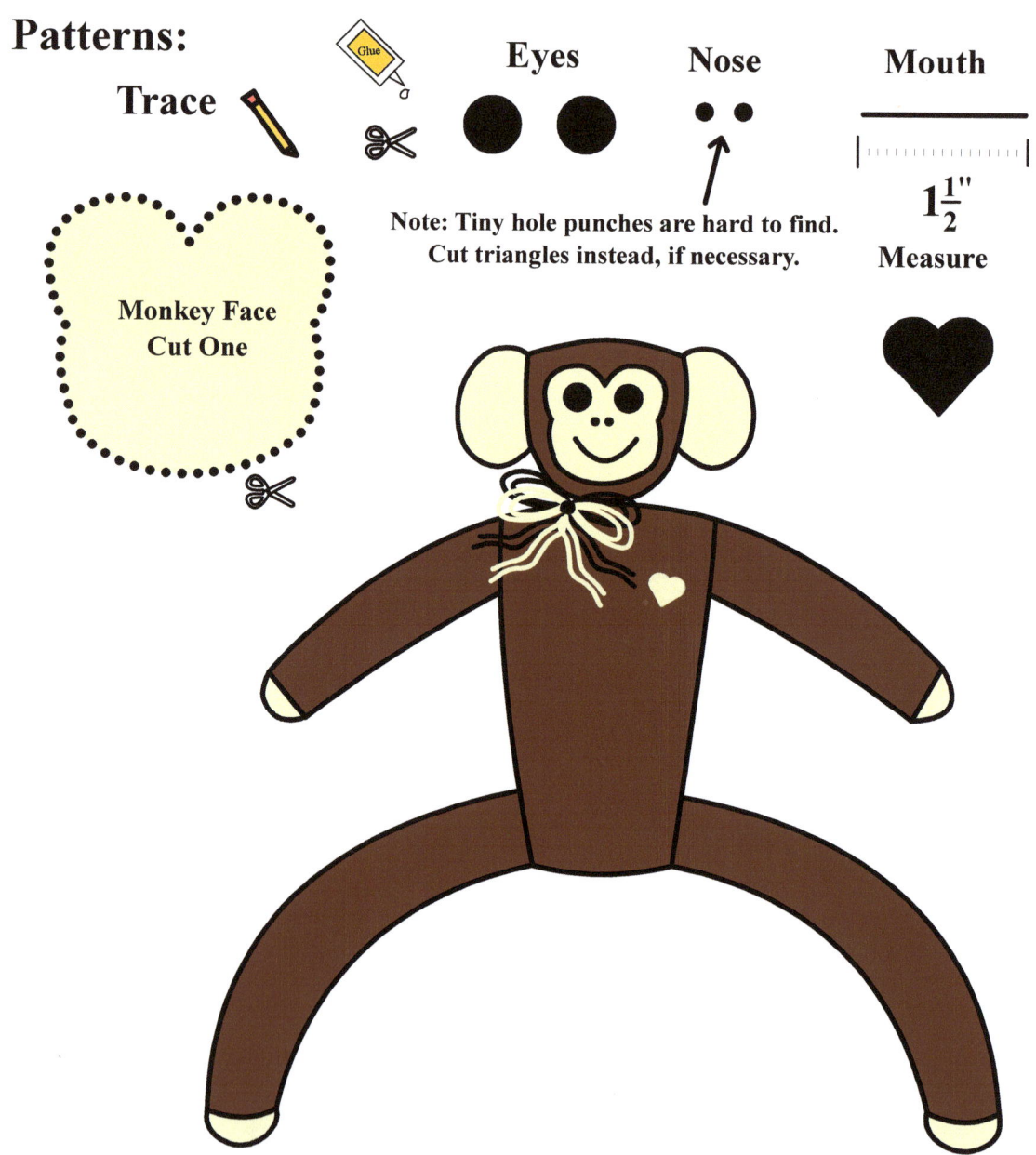

Warning: Keep sharp objects, small materials and rubber bands away from babies and small children.

Tortoise Factoids

- The tortoise is a reptile and a land dweller. It is also known as a land turtle.
- Female tortoises lay their eggs at night in nesting burrows which they cover with soil, leaves and grasses.
- Depending on the species, the eggs take 60 to 120 days to hatch.
- As herbivores, tortoises eat some fruits, grasses, leaves, clover, some insects, weeds and leafy vegetables. Only the proper kind and size pellets should be fed to tortoises because the wrong size can cause choking and death.
- Some tortoises can live as long as 150 years or more. One famous tortoise lived to be 188 years old, and another was claimed to have lived to be 250 years old.
- Female tortoises have short, down-turned tails. Male tortoises have longer tails, which curve off to one side.
- Desert tortoise spends 95 percent of its life in underground burrows and can live in temperatures of 140 degrees Fahrenheit or more. A tortoise can have several dozen burrows in their territory.
- Desert tortoises grunt, hiss and make popping sounds and fight for dominance.
- There is a famous fable called *The Tortoise and the Hare* which tells of a hare that ridicules a slow-moving tortoise. The tortoise challenges the hare to a race. The hare accepts and is so confident of winning the race that he stops to take a nap along the way. However, when he awakes, he finds the tortoise slowly crawling over the finish line. The moral of the fable is: Slow and steady wins the race!

TerryGami Tortoise Instructions

Materials:

*Two thin, green, terrycloth washcloths approximately 12" x 12"
*Two medium rubber bands, green (optional) plus a few extra
*Needle and matching thread
*Clear fabric or craft glue (non-toxic and non-flammable)
*Black ribbon 12" x 1/4" for neck bow
*Black yarn 30" for trimming the legs and the shell
*Black foam board for eyes and nails
*Round hole punch for the eyes 1/4"
*Heart hole punch 1/4" for nails and eyes for girl tortoise
*Quilt batting
*Scissors
*Ruler

Finished Size: Approximately 5 1/2" w x 5 1/2" l x 3" h

1. Cut the tags off of the cloths, and then place them flat on a flat surface in a diamond shape. Roll the opposite corners to the center of each cloth.

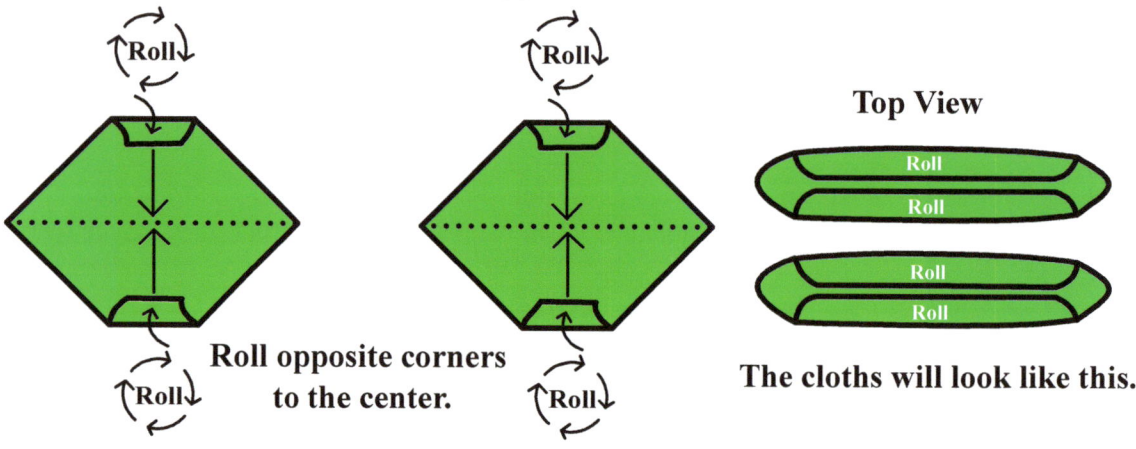

Roll opposite corners to the center.

Top View

The cloths will look like this.

2. Stack the two cloths with the rolls on the bottom cloth facing down and the rolls of the top cloth facing up. Measure down 6 inches on each end, and then wrap rubber bands.

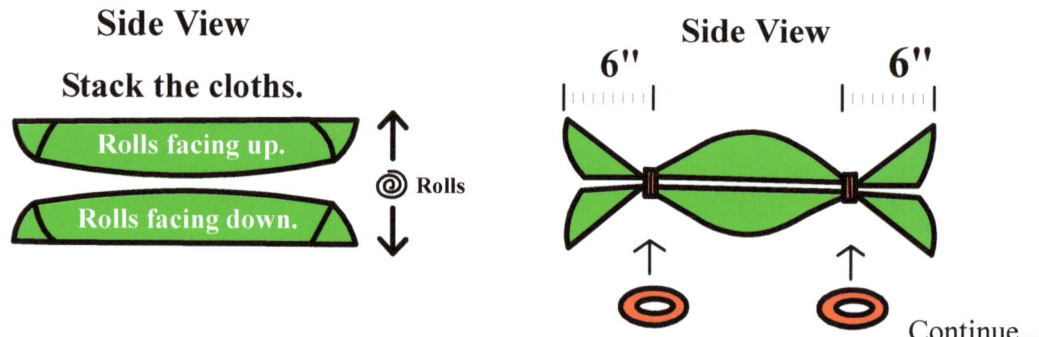

Continue...

TerryGami Tortoise Instructions

3. Open the whole between the cloths.

A side view showing the rolls facing the outside.

---

4. Turn the cloths inside out so that the roll are now facing each other on the inside, and the corners are on the inside, too.

Turn the cloths inside out. **The rolls and corners will now be on the inside.** **The corners fill up the entire hole.**

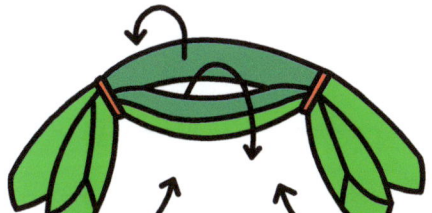 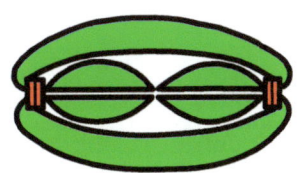 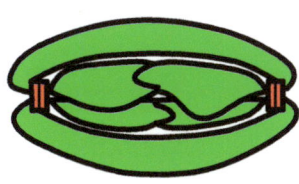

---

5. Pull the corners out, one on each side. Turn the ensemble so one side is the shell on the top, and the other side is the stomach on the bottom. It doesn't matter which side is which.

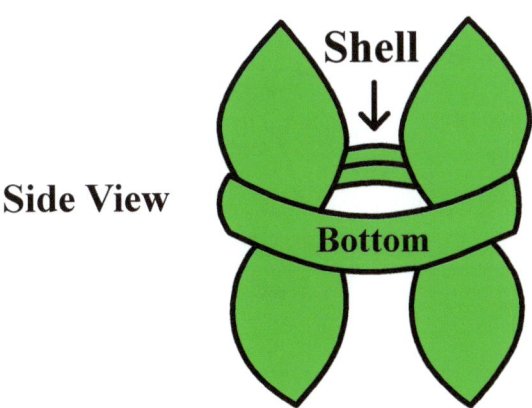

Side View

Continue...

TerryGami Tortoise Instructions

6. **To form the head:** Roll the stomach side (or bottom) forward 1 inches and then wrap a rubber band at the 1 inch point.

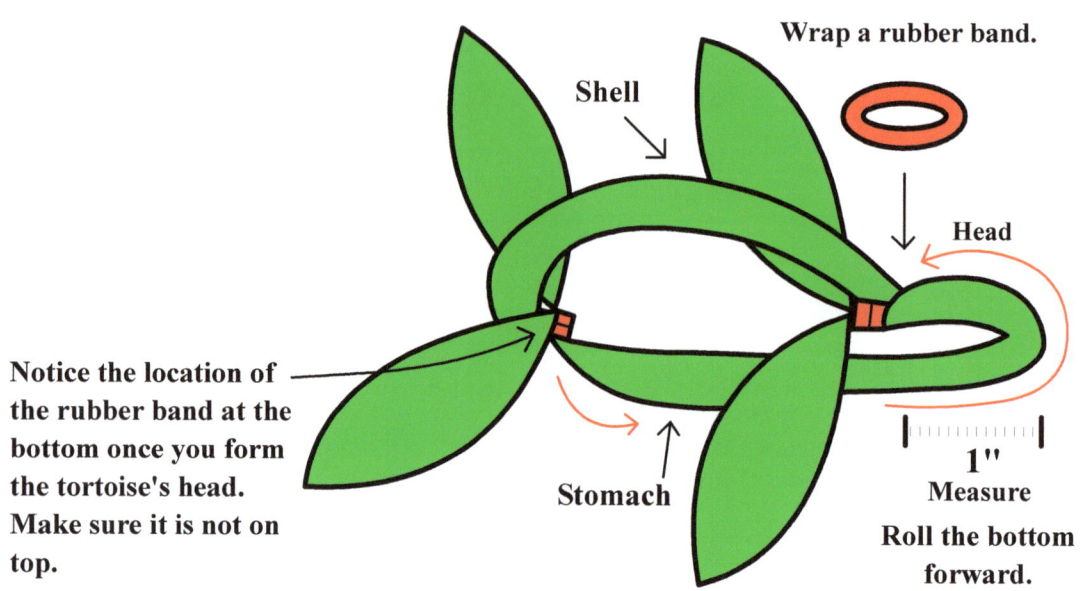

7. Unwind the rolls in the center of the body, both top and bottom, but not all of the way. Add the stuffing, filling the spaces between the rolls, both on the top and the bottom.

Continue...

TerryGami Tortoise Instrucitons

8. Stuff the head. Fold the corners of the legs under, and then re-roll the legs. Sew or glue the legs closed. To form a knee: Bend at the center of the leg and then sew or glue under the crease. Sew or glue the sides of the body closed. Cover the rubber bands by the shoulders with material from the shell, and then sew. If making a turtle, fold over the corner, stuff it, and sew it closed.

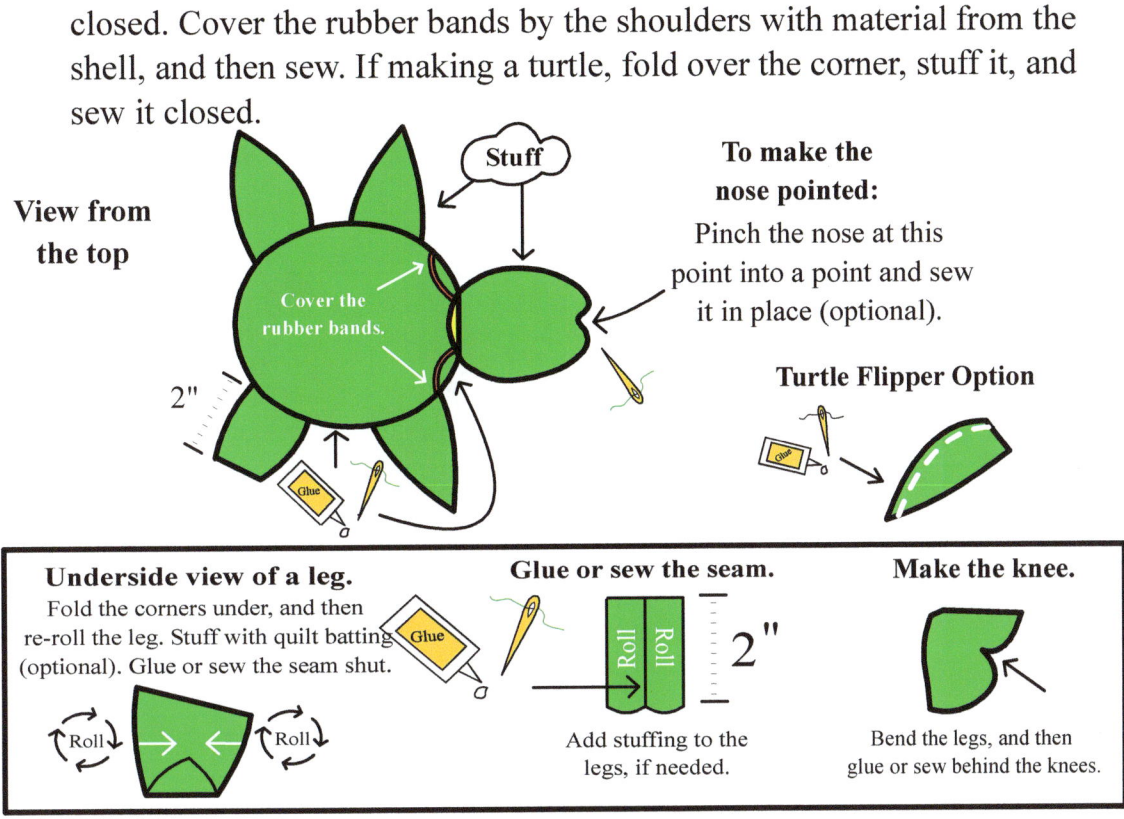

9. Prepare and glue on the eyes, mouth, nails and tail. Cut six or eight hearts or triangles for the nails. Use the hole punch for the eyes.

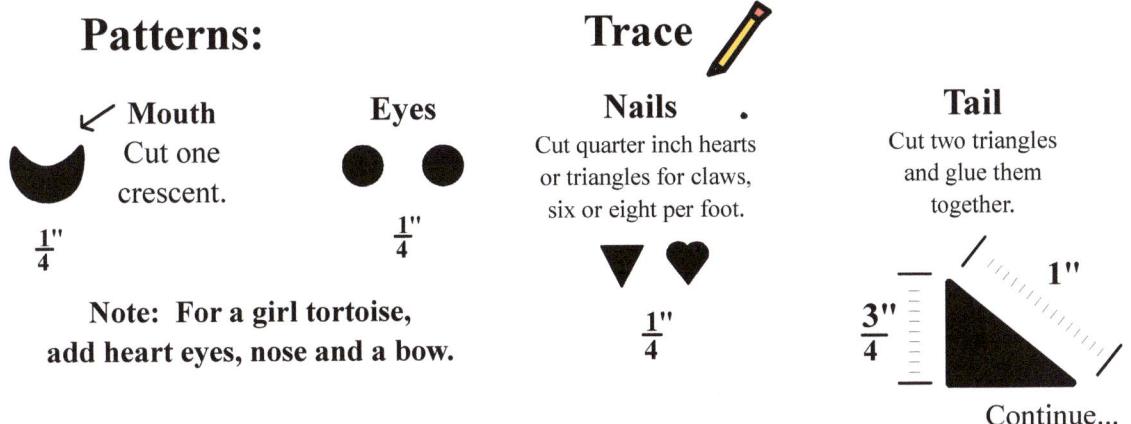

Continue...

35

TerryGami Tortoise Instructions

10. Sew or glue the yarn around the shell and legs. Glue on the facial features, claws/nails, and tail. Tie on the ribbon.

Boy Tortoise

11. Trim any snags.

Girl Tortoise

Warning: Keep sharp tools, small materials and rubber bands away from infants and small children.

Hare Factoids

- Hares give birth to young that can see and have hair, unlike rabbits. Consequently, the young are self-sufficient sooner than baby rabbits are.
- Hares are very fast and can run up to 45 miles per hour. They move by jumping rather than running.
- Unlike rabbits, hares do not live in groups, although they may live in pairs.
- Hares live above ground in shallow, grass nests called forms. Females use their own hair to make nests for their young.
- Compared to rabbits, hares have longer ears and tails, and larger bodies. They have black markings on their coats.
- Hares feed on leaves, bark and grasses, which are difficult to digest. This is why hares and rabbits eat their own droppings so the food passes twice through the digestive system. This trait is similar to cows chewing their cud.
- In the spring, during the mating season, hares can be seen boxing and fighting. This is no doubt where the phrase "madder than a March hare" came from.
- There is a famous fable called *The Tortoise and the Hare* which tells of a hare that ridicules a slow-moving tortoise. The tortoise challenges the hare to a race. The hare accepts and is so confident of winning the race that he stops to take a nap along the way. However, when he awakes, he finds the tortoise slowly crawling over the finish line. The moral of the fable is: Slow and steady wins the race!

TerryGami Hare Instructions

Materials:
* Two thin, terrycloth washcloths approximately 12" x 12"
* Small pieces of black foam board or 3 pom poms for the eyes
* Three medium rubber bands
* Clear fabric glue or needle and thread (non-toxic and non-flammable)
* Needle or thread
* Yarn (12") or ribbon (12" x 1/4")
* Tatting thread or floss, 6" for whiskers
* Large cotton ball
* Round and heart hole puncher, 1/4 " if using foam board for facial features
* Scissors
* Ruler

Finished size: Approximately 6" x 6"

1. Cut off the tags, and then place both cloths flat on a flat surface in a diamond shape. Roll opposite corners to the center on each cloth.

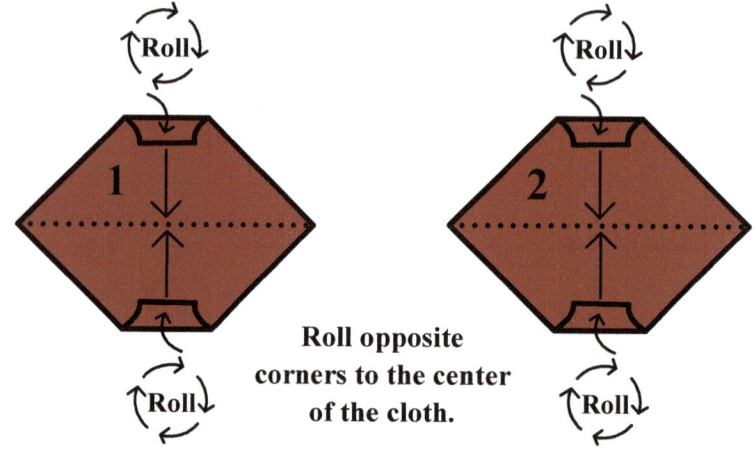

Roll opposite corners to the center of the cloth.

2. Both cloths should look like this. Stack the two cloths with the bottom rolls facing down and the top rolls facing up.

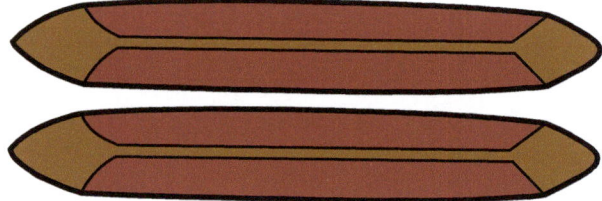

Stack two of the cloths.

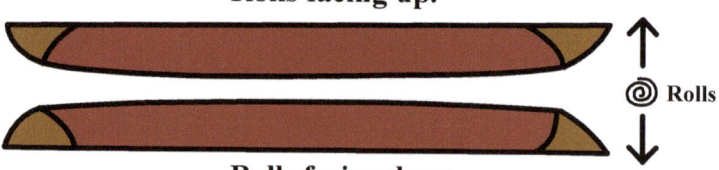

Rolls facing up.

Rolls facing down.

↑ ⓞ Rolls ↓

Continue...

TerryGami Hare Instructions

3. Measure down four inches on one end, and then wrap a rubber band.

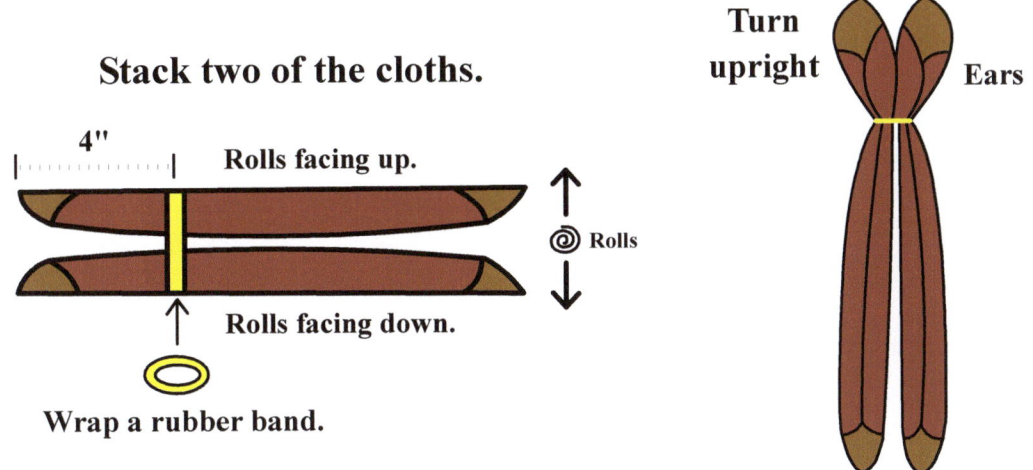

4. **To form the head: A)** Turn each side below the rubber band so that the rolls face toward the back. Note the directions of the arrows in Step **A**. **B)** Measure down 2 inches, and then wrap a rubber band. **C)** Measure up 7 inches from the bottom corners, and then wrap a rubber band to begin forming the legs and body.

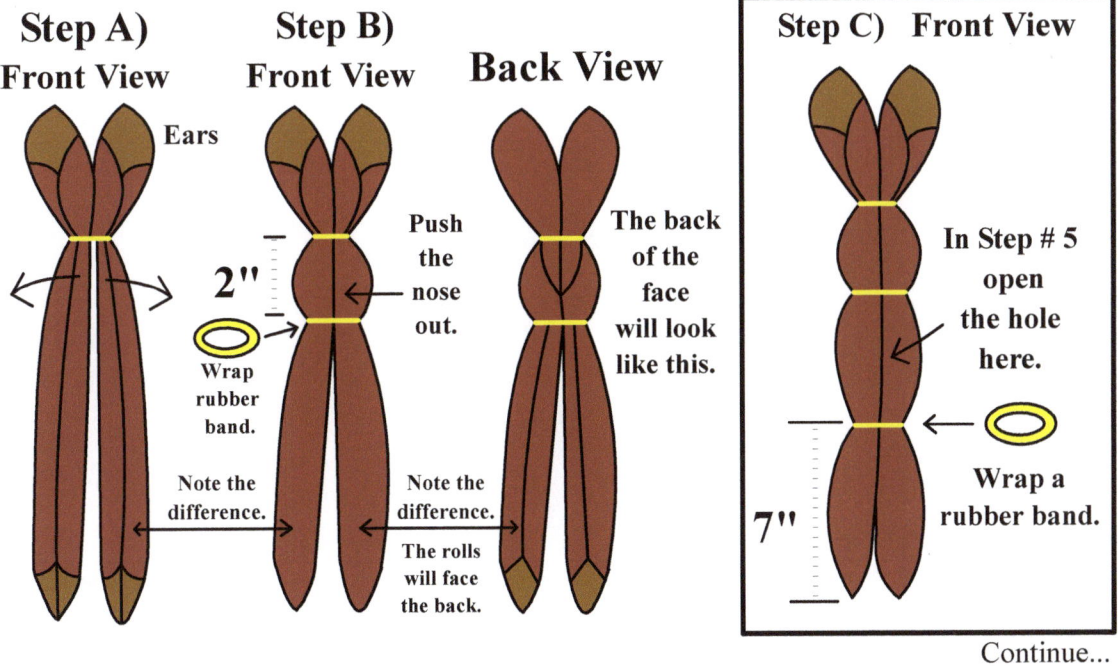

Continue...

TerryGami Hare Instructions

5. **A)** Open the hole between the two cloths, and then **B)** pull the bottom corners through the back of the hole to form the body and the legs. **C)** Note where to place the cotton ball tail. When you glue the tail on, make sure it covers the rubber band.

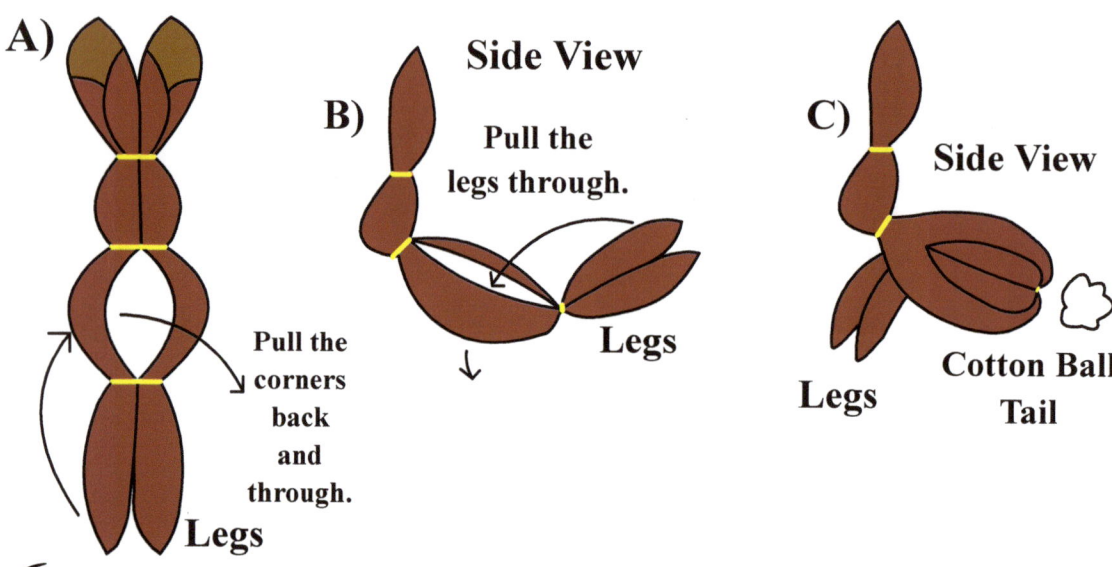

6. Fold the corners of the legs under to the desired lengh (1 1/2 inches), and then re-roll each leg. Sew or glue the seams closed. For details, see the box.

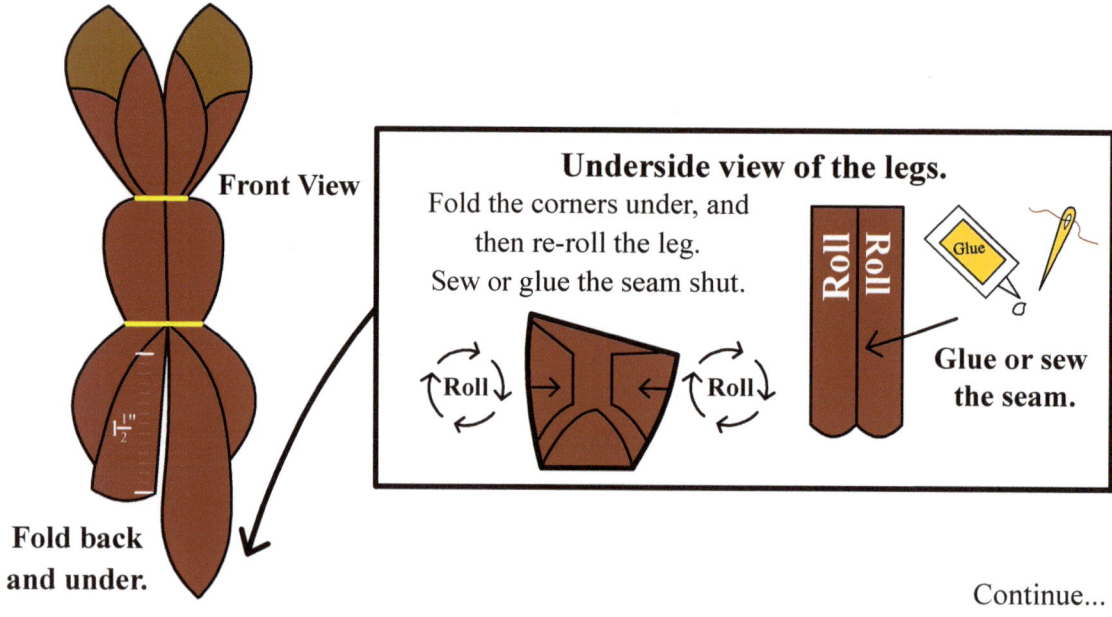

Continue...

40

TerryGami Hare Instructions

7. At the bottom of the ears, pull down the material over the rubber band, and then sew or glue it down to cover it. Prepare the facial features. Glue on the eyes, nose and whiskers. Tie a bow around the neck. Tie yarn around each leg (optional). Glue on the cotton ball tail. Trim any snags on the material.

Patterns: Trace the patterns or use a hole punch.

Nose
Eyes
Cut Whiskers $\frac{3"}{4}$

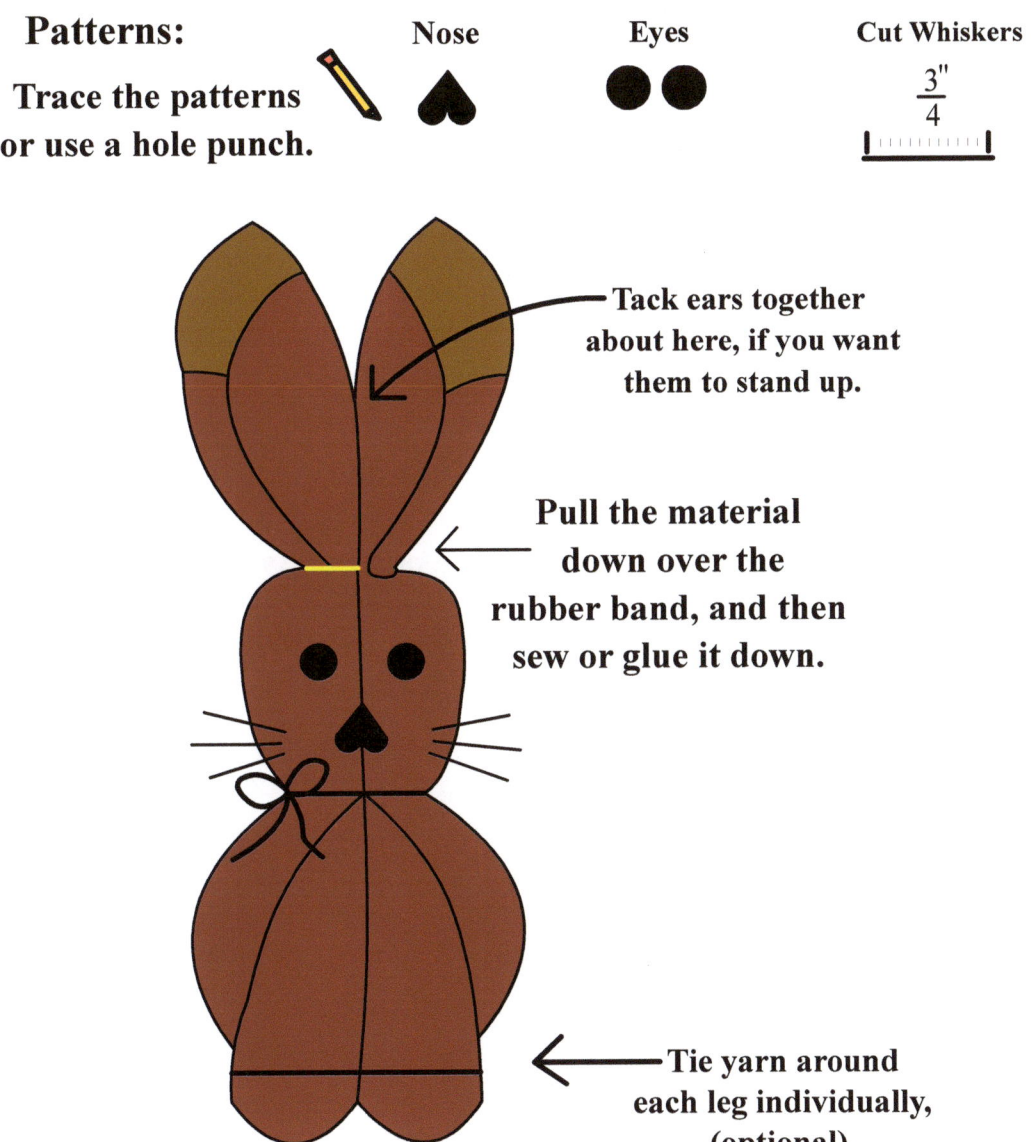

- Tack ears together about here, if you want them to stand up.
- Pull the material down over the rubber band, and then sew or glue it down.
- Tie yarn around each leg individually, (optional).

Warning: Keep sharp tools, small materials and rubber bands away from infants and small children.

Duck Factoids

- Duck is the common name for several species in the Anatidae family of birds.
- Ducks are for the most part aquatic and are found in sea water and fresh water.
- Ducks eat aquatic plants and grasses, small amphibians, worms, fish and mollusks.
- Duck have a variety of calls: cooing, grunts, yodels and whistles.
- The phase "a sitting duck" has come to mean "an easy target" because ducks floating on water or squatting on land cannot move quickly enough to fly from these positions.
- While adult ducks can fly fast, they can be caught easily on water by fish such as the pike and the muskie.
- Other predators of ducks include birds of prey such as falcons.
- The word duck comes from Old English which means diver.
- The word duck or hen is usually used when referring to the female of the species.
- The word drake is used when referring to adult male ducks.
- Only female ducks quack.

TerryGami Duck Instructions

Materials:
*Two thin, yellow washcloths approximately 12"x 12"
*One thin, orange washcloth approximately 12"x12"
*Needle and matching thread
*Clear fabric glue (non-toxic and non-flammable)
*Black foam board for the eyes
*Ribbon 1/4" x 12"
*Two medium rubber bands
*Hole Punch 1/4" (for the eyes)
*Scissors
*Ruler

Finished size: Approximately 4"h x 9"l.

1. Cut the tags off of the cloths, and then place all three cloths flat on a flat surface in a diamond shape (one at a time). **A)** Measure down 4 inches from the corner on the orange cloth. Mark the cloth at the 4-inch point, and then cut the corner off. **B)** Place the beak piece on top of the top corner of one of the yellow cloths, and then roll the opposite corner until the beak measures about one inch long. **C)** With the remaining yellow cloth, roll the opposite corners to the center. This cloth will be the body of the duck.

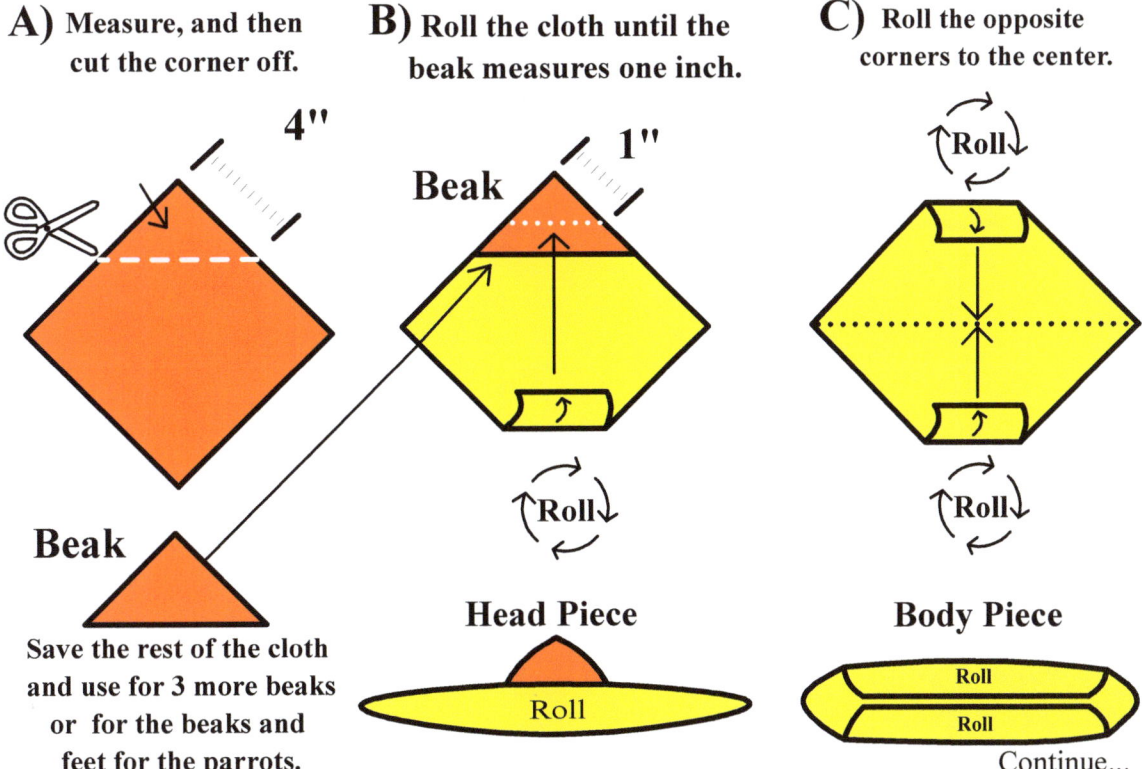

A) Measure, and then cut the corner off.

B) Roll the cloth until the beak measures one inch.

C) Roll the opposite corners to the center.

Save the rest of the cloth and use for 3 more beaks or for the beaks and feet for the parrots.

Continue...

43

TerryGami Duck Instructions

2. Fold the head piece cloth (the one with the beak) in half with the roll on the top. Adjust the beak, making sure the top and bottom of the beak are straight. Wrap a rubber band under the beak to form the head of the duck. Turn to the back of the head piece, then trim off any remenants of the orange beak piece that may be showing. Sew or glue the flaps on either side closed.

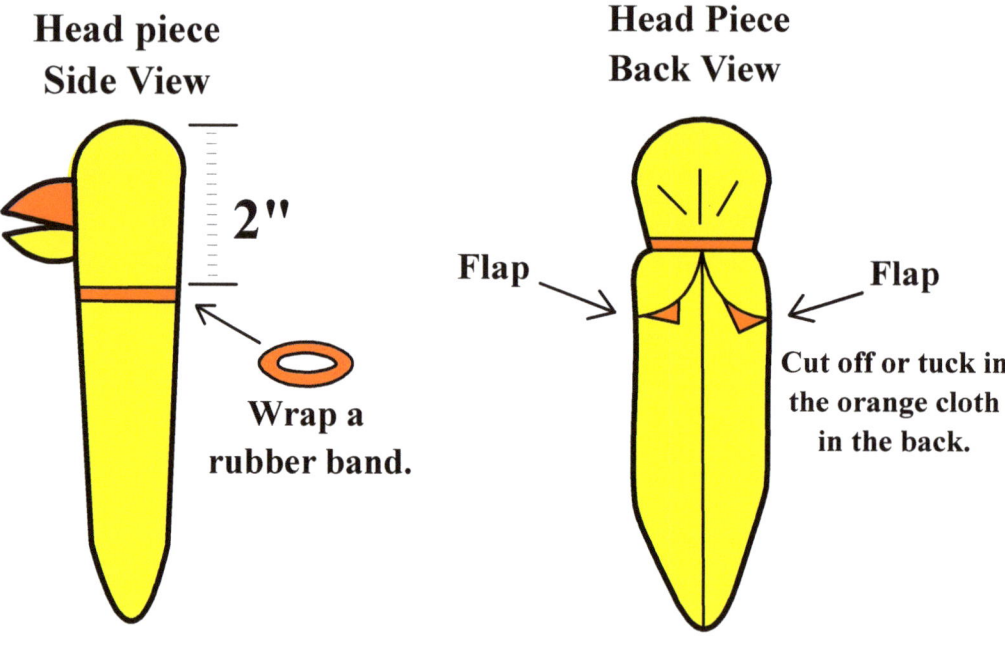

3. Fold the second yellow cloth in half with the rolls on the inside.

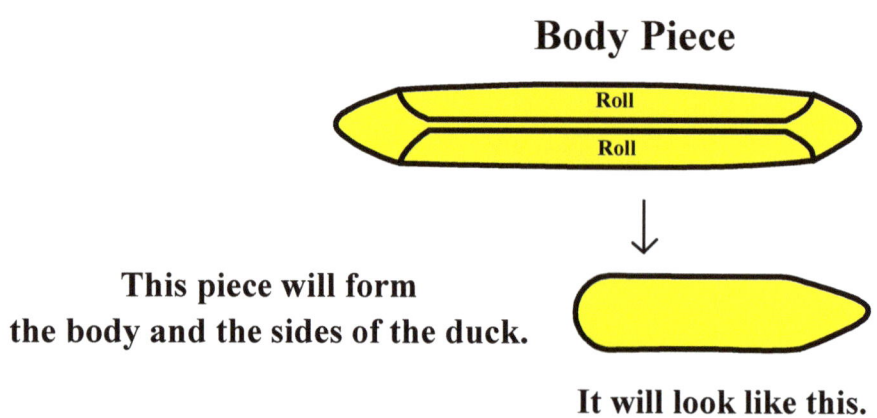

Continue...

TerryGami Duck Instructions

4. Curve the bottom part of the head piece back behind the head. Now place the head piece between the fold of the body piece. See the view from the top. The rolls of the body piece face the head piece. Make sure the tail ends are even.

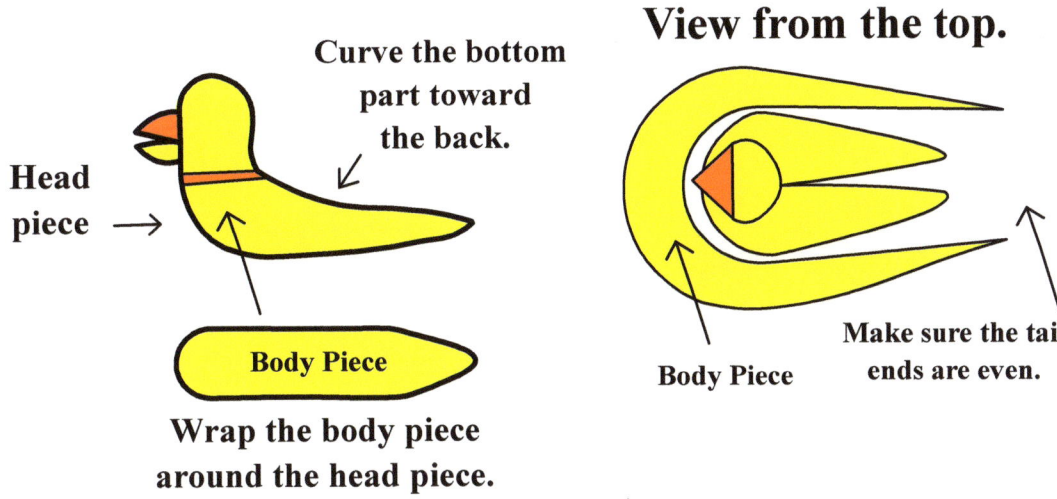

5. Measure 4 inches from the end of the tail, and then wrap a rubber band at this point. Sew or glue the body piece to the head piece. Bring the two sides of the body piece together over the back and sew or glue together. Cut the rubber band off of the neck. Gather and sew or glue the tail together, and then take or cut the rubber band off of the tail (optional).

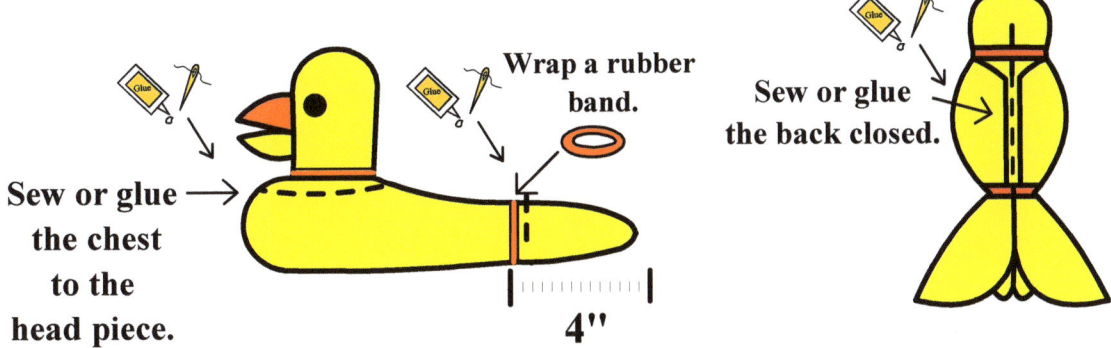

Continue...

TerryGami Duck Instructions

6. Prepare the eyes, using a hole punch or trace and cut out. Glue on the eyes. Cut the rubber band from around the neck (optional). Tie the ribbon in a bow around the neck.

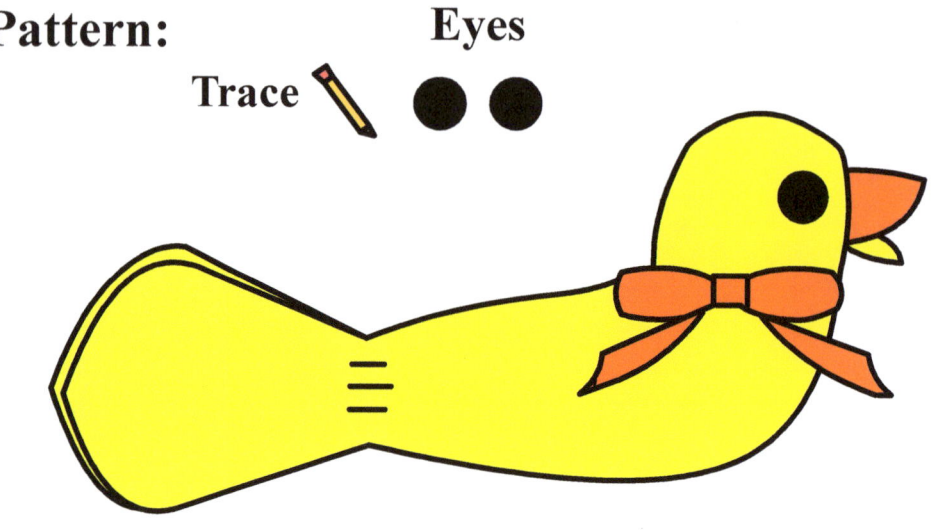

Pattern: **Eyes**
Trace

7. Trim any snags. There are many other colors for ducks: green, black, or white. Also, the body can be one color and the head another color.

Warning: Keep sharp objects, small materials and rubber bands away from babies and small children.

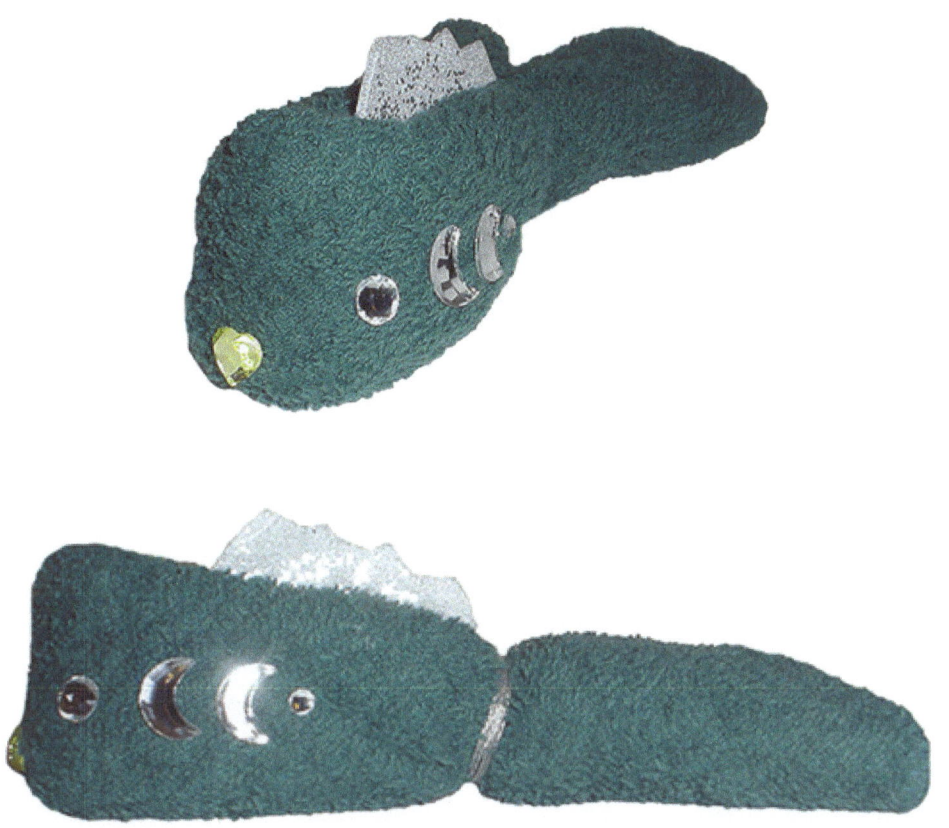

Fish Factoids

- Fish are fin and gill-bearing vertebrate animals, which do not have limbs with fingers or digits and live in water. They are covered with scales and have two sets of paired fins, one or two dorsal fins, a fin tail and anal fin.
- Fish are cold-blooded animals. This means that their body temperature is controlled through external means and that they are dependant on the environment for their heat source.
- Fish lay eggs rather than bear their young live.
- The smallest fish is the Philippine goby, which is 1/3 inch long, and the largest fish is the whale shark, which is 65 feet in length.
- Some species of fish can fly or glide through the air, and some can walk on land like the spotted perch.
- Fish predate dinosaurs and have been on the earth for more than 450 million years.

TerryGami Fish Instructions

Materials:
*One green or grey terrycloth washcloth appoximately 12" x 12"
*One medium sized rubber band
*Clear fabric craft glue (non-toxic and non-flammable)
*Small pieces of silver glitter foam board or one piece of plain with glitter on each side for the fin
*Clear craft jewels, 4 crescent, two 1/4" round shaped, two 1/8" round shaped, one 1/4" heart (or sequins)
*Scissors
*Ruler

Note: No sewing necessary unless you want to sew the bottom of the fish closed.

Finished size: Approximately 8"l x 3 1/2"h.

1. Cut off the tag, and then place the cloth flat on a flat surface in a diamond shape. Roll the opposite corners to the center of the cloth.

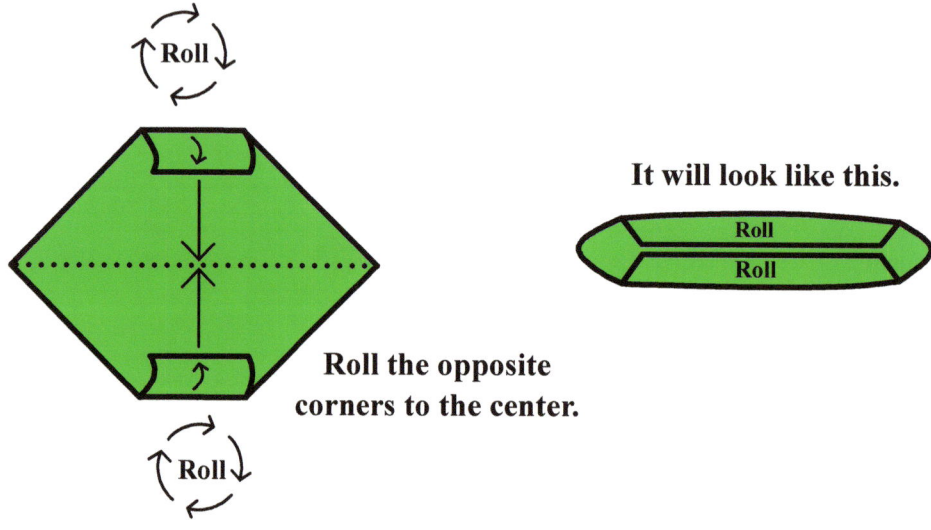

It will look like this.

Roll the opposite corners to the center.

2. **A)** Fold the cloth in half with the rolls on the inside. **B)** Measure down 4 inches from the corners, gathering the material before you wrap the rubber band.

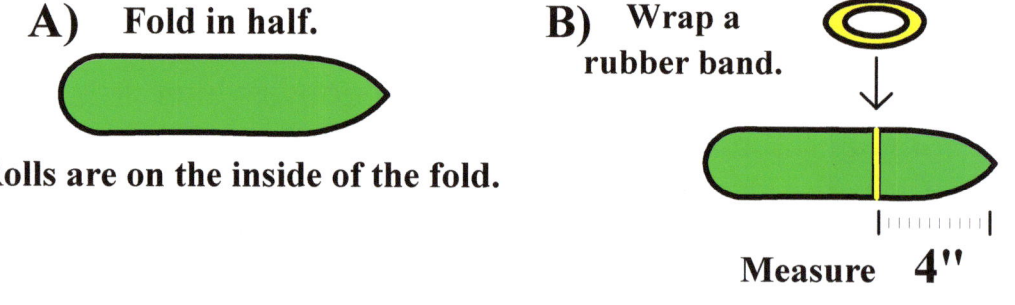

A) Fold in half.

Rolls are on the inside of the fold.

B) Wrap a rubber band.

Measure **4"**

Continue...

TerryGami Fish Instructions

3. Cover the rubber band with ribbon or yarn.

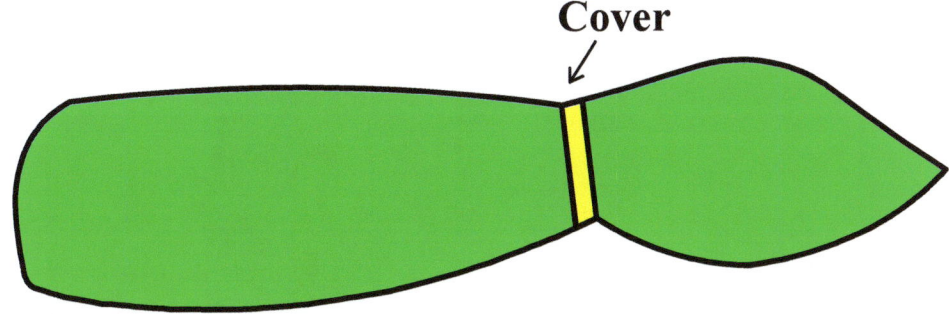

4. Prepare the eyes, gills, mouth and fin. Cut two fins, and glue the sticky sides together. (Cut one non-sticky back foam board and glue glitter to both sides.) Glue on the eyes, fin, and gills to both sides of the fish, and glue the heart mouth to the front of the fish.

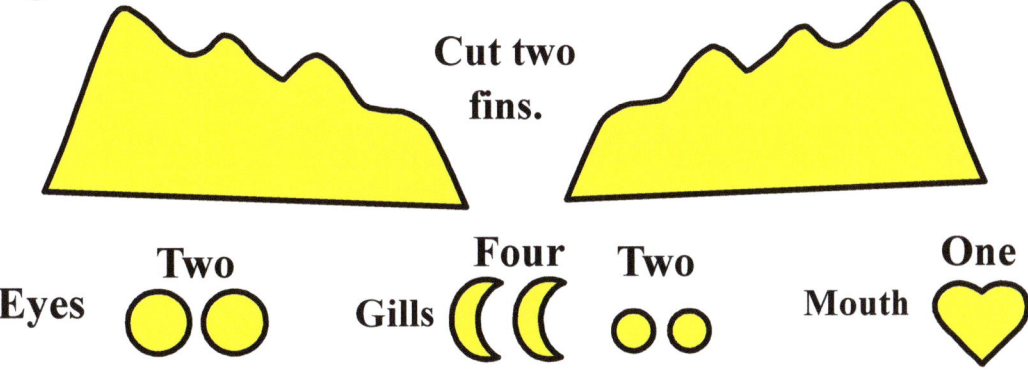

5. Trim any snags in the material.

Warning: Keep sharp tools, small materials and rubber bands away from infants and small children.

Pirate Captain's Parrot

- Most parrots are multi-colored birds although some are white or black.
- Parrots are found in the tropical Southern Hemisphere of the world.
- Parrots have upright bodies, long, strong beaks and strong claws.
- Male and female parrots are usually similar in appearance.
- Some parrots can imitate human voices and words. The African Grey parrot can have a vocabulary of up to 10,000 words.
- It is said that some parrots have the intelligence of a two year old, and some even have the intelligence a five-year-old human being.
- Parrots eat nuts, flower buds, plant material, seeds, fruit and meat or carrion.

TerryGami Captain's Parrot Instructions

Materials

*One green, one blue, one red and one orange terrycloth washcloths approximately 12" x 12"
*A piece of white felt for the skull & crossbone or foam board cut out of skull & crossbone
*One black (1/2) felt piece for the hat
*Three medium rubber bands
*One corner of a red bandana
*One black, 1/4" acrylic gem for the eye (a black felt patch will serve as the other eye)
*Hair clip to clip parrot on shoulder (optional)
*Red ribbon 1/2" x 8" or use a strip of bandana
*Needle and matching thread (green and orange)
*Tatting thread measure it so it is long enough to be tied around the head (approx.10")
*Quilt batting or fiberfil
*Clear fabric glue (non-toxic and non-flammable)
*One gold or silver craft earring with one gold bead on it
*A 2-inch strip of Velcro® to attach the parrot to the shoulder of a shirt (optional)
*Scissors
*Ruler

Finished size: Approximately 12"h x 4"w.

1. Place the green cloth flat on a flat surface in a diamond shape. Roll the top corner to the center, and then roll the bottom corner to the center. Turn it over so it doesn't unroll.

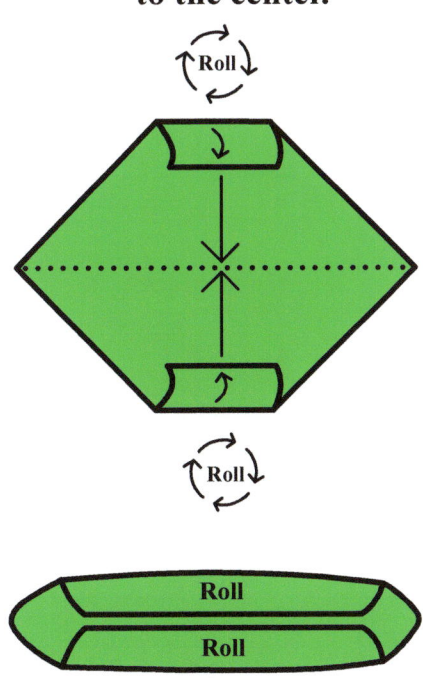

Roll opposite corners to the center.

Continue...

TerryGami Captain's Parrot Instructions

2. Place the blue and red cloths flat on a flat surface in a diamond shape. Measure up 4 inches from the bottom corner on each cloth, and then roll up to the 4-inch point. Roll the top corner to meet the bottom corner on each cloth. Turn the cloths over so they don't unroll.

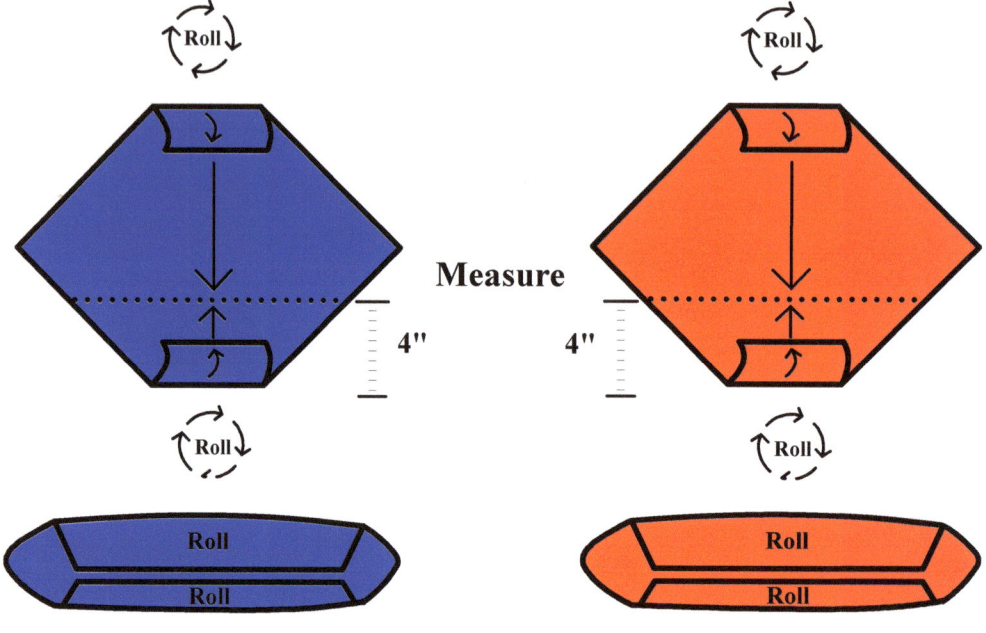

3. **A)** With the rolls on the inside, fold the green cloth with one side 2 inches longer on one side. **B)** Turn the cloth so that the flat, smooth side faces you. **C)** Measure down two inches from the fold, and then wrap a rubber band.

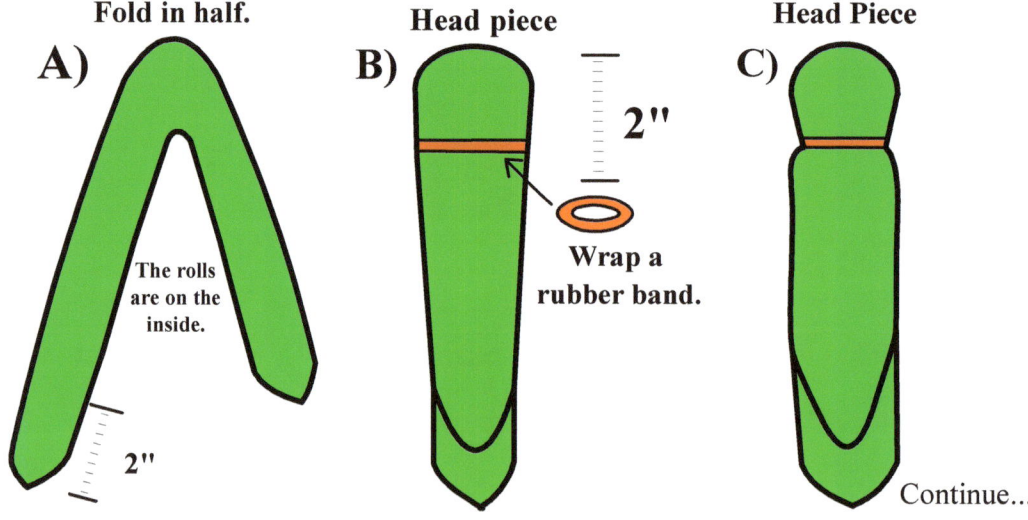

Continue...

TerryGami Captain's Parrot Instructions

4. Stuff and round out the head piece. Round out the head. Open up the bottom sides.

Head Piece

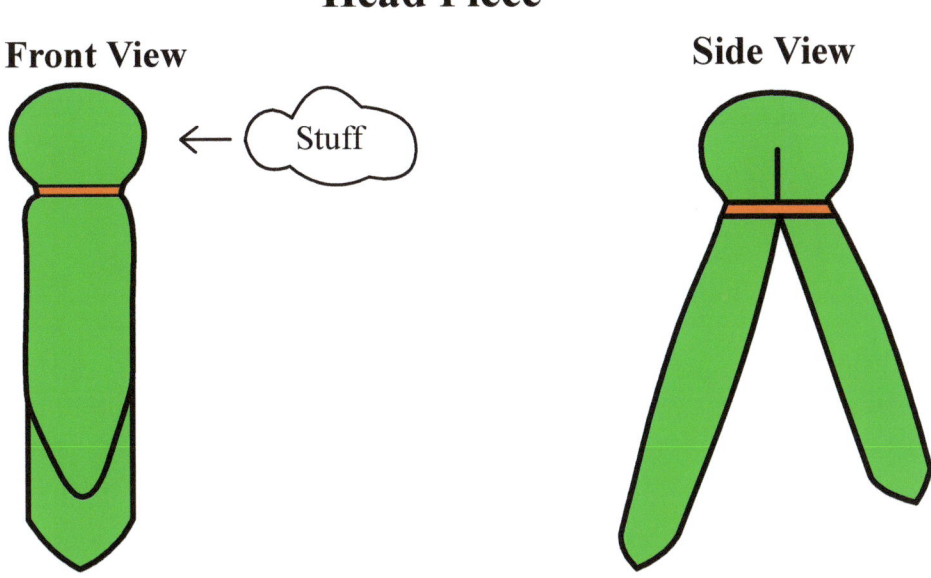

---

5. **A)** Fold the blue cloth in half with the rolls on the inside, making sure the ends are even. **B)** Place the head piece over the fold of the blue body piece. **C)** The front view will look like this.

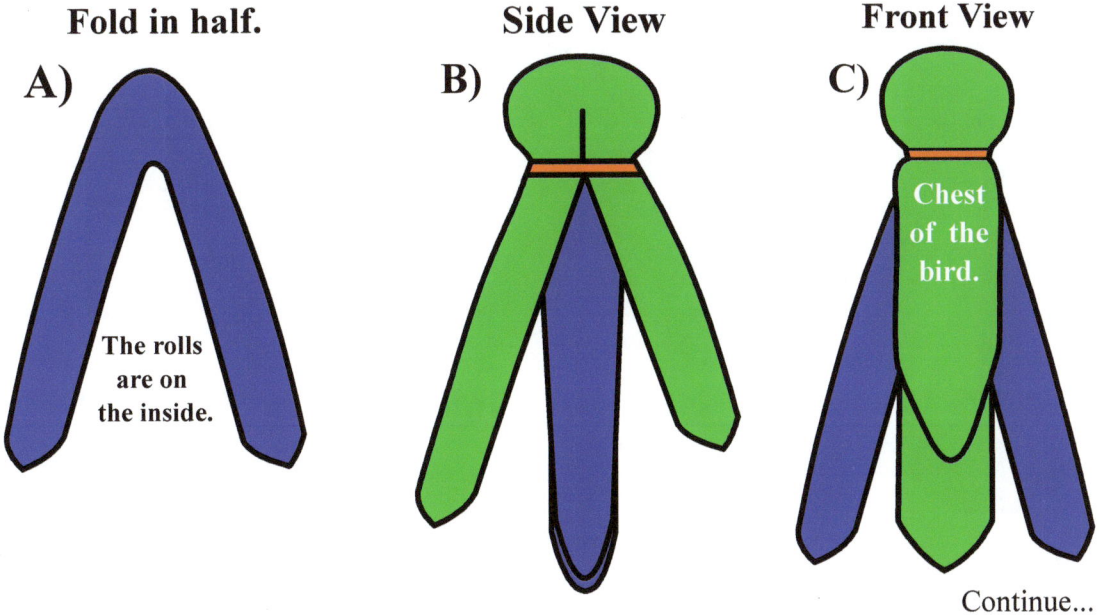

Continue...

TerryGami Captain's Parrot Instructions

6. **A)** Fold the red cloth in half with the rolls on the inside. **B)** Wrap a rubber band about 1 or 2 inches down from the fold. This will be part of the body and tail feathers.

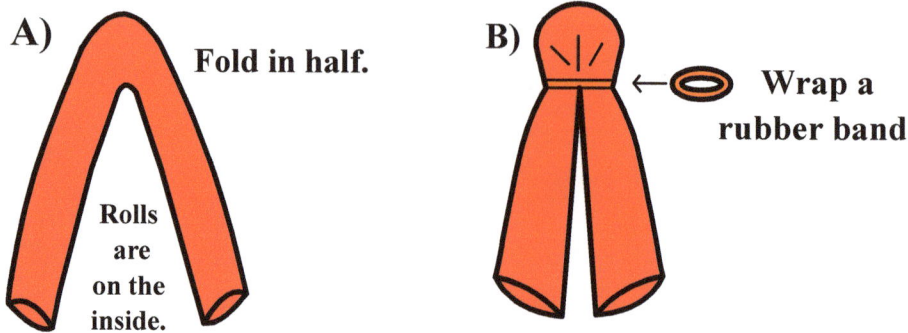

7. **A)** Pull up the green cloth on the front side, and then lay the red cloth in between the blue cloth. **B)** Cover the fold of the red cloth with the blue cloth slightly on each side to form the shoulders/wings of the bird. Make sure the tail feathers (the ends of the red and blue cloths) are facing in the direction shown in the illustration. **C) To form the chest:** Bring the green cloth back down in front to cover the red cloth, and then wrap a rubber band about 3 1/2 inches down from the rubber band around the neck.

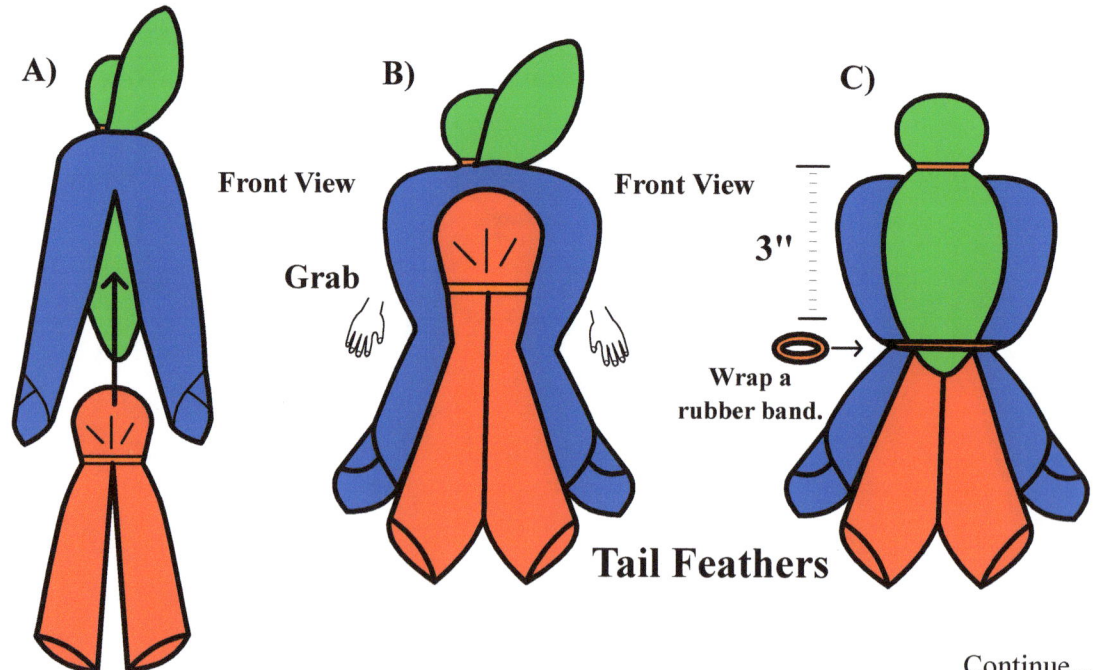

Continue...

TerryGami Captain's Parrot Instructions

8. **To make the feet:** **A)** Place the orange cloth flat on a flat surface. Measure down about 1 1/2 inch from two of the corners, mark them off, and then cut the corner off. **B)** Fold the side corners over so the piece measures about 3/4 of an inch, and then **C)** roll the rough edges to the end of the corner. Trim to fit the parrot, if necessary.

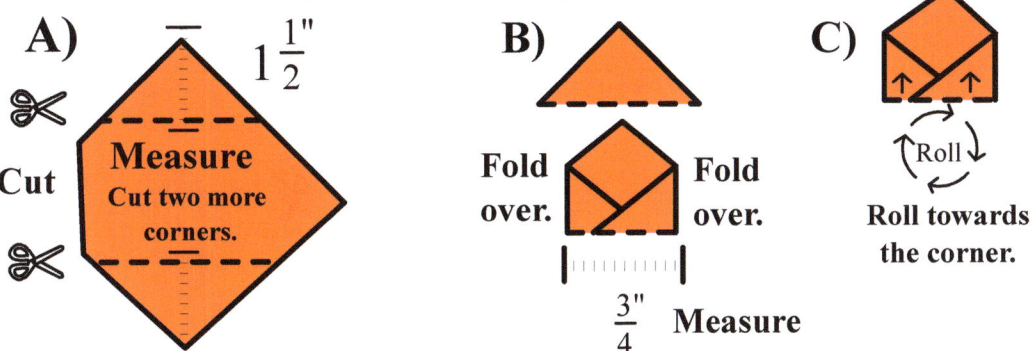

Using the whip stitch, sew the edges together, but as you sew and reach the first 1/4-inch mark, wrap the thread around the entire piece creating a toe. Sew another 1/4 inch, and then wrap the thread around the piece at this point, creating the last two toes. Sew the seam side of the piece to one side of the green corner which extends below the rubber band, leaving enough room for the other foot. Repeat this step for the second foot, and then attach them.

Note: If you want the foot to curve a bit, sew a running stitch through the entire length of the back and pull the thread tight, and then tie off the thread.

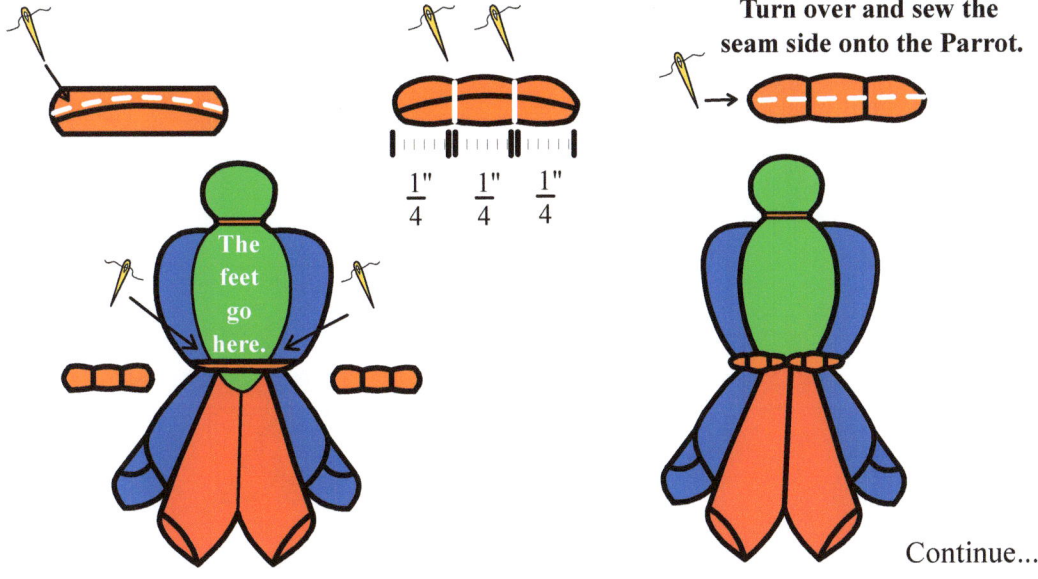

Continue...

TerryGami Captain's Parrot Instructions

9. **To make the beak:** A) Measure down 1 1/2 inches from one of the corners on the orange cloth, mark it, and then cut the corner off. B) Cut about 1/4 inch off each side of the corner. C) Fold over the rough edge about 1/2 inch, D) and then roll each side to the middle. E) Sew or glue the rolls together, tapering the beak at the corner end. F) Turn over, and then sew or glue the beak to the face about 1 1/4 inch from the top of the head. Sew down the end of the beak so it curves a bit.

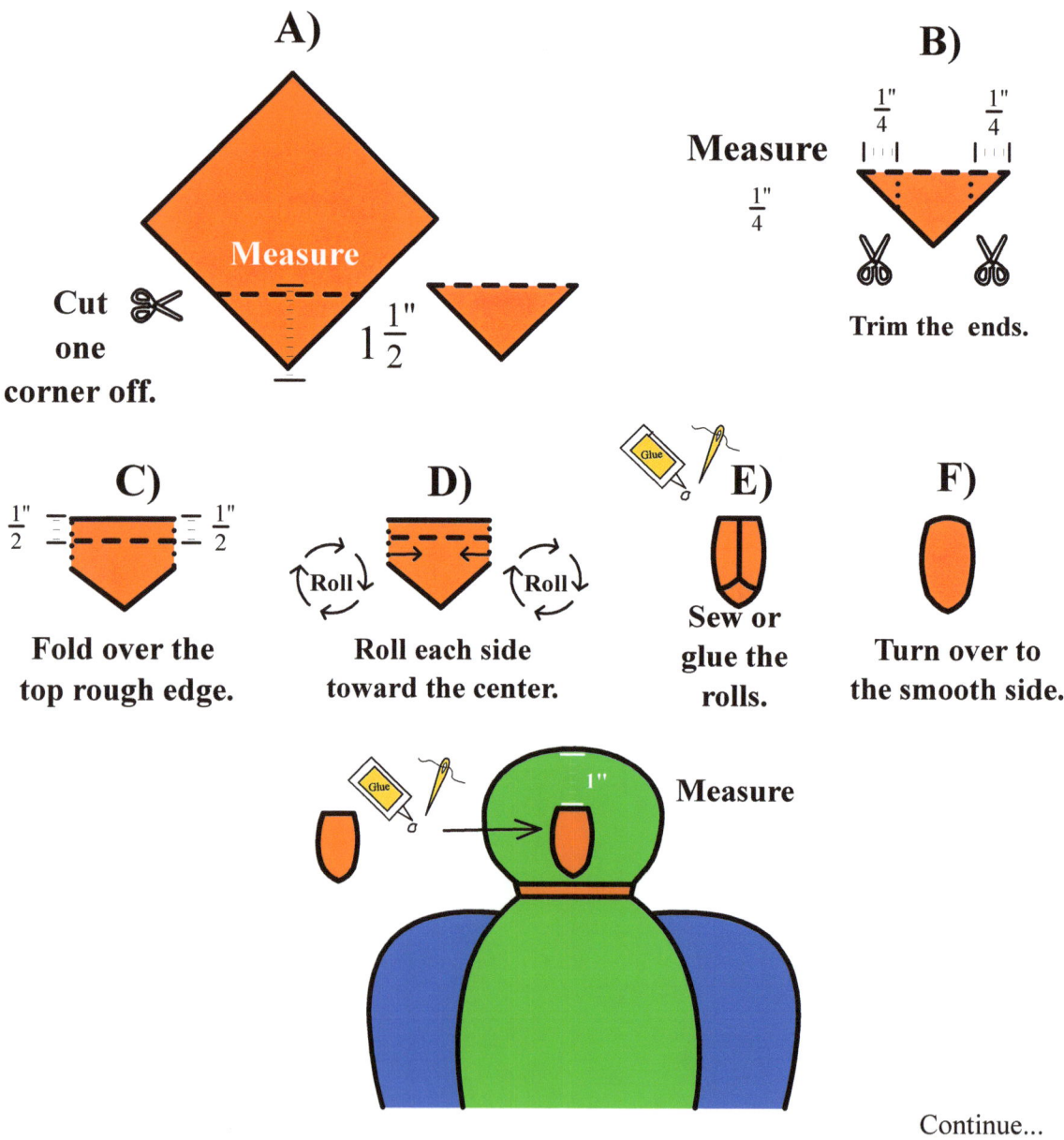

Continue...

TerryGami Captain's Parrot Instructions

10. Make a pattern for the hat, and the skull and crossbones from paper. Pin the hat pattern to the black felt square, and then cut it out. Pin the skull and crossbone to the white felt, and then cut it out. Cut the slit in the top of the hat. Glue on the skull and crossbones to the hat. The head will be covered with a bandana.

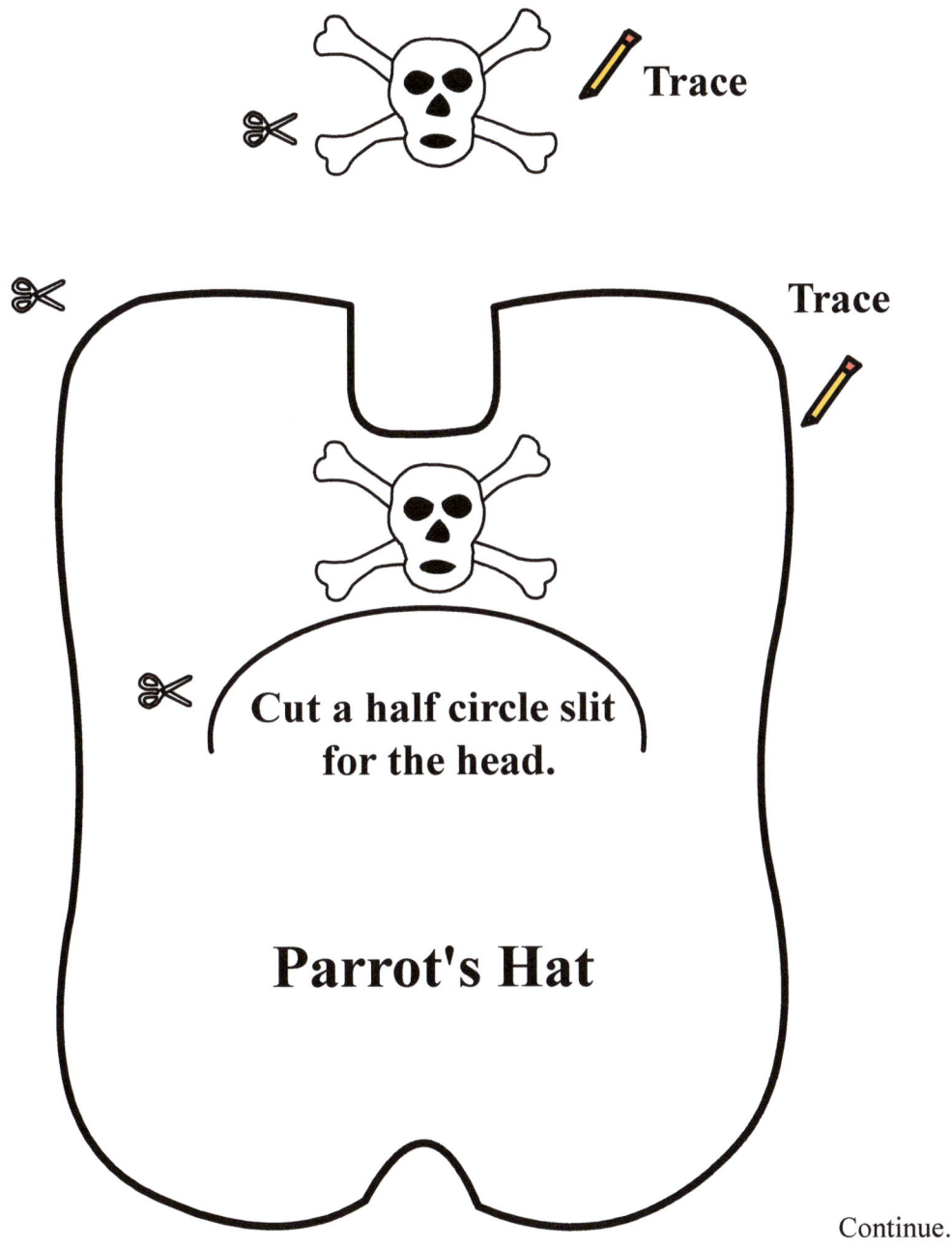

Continue...

11. TerryGami Captain's Parrot Instructions

For the eye patch, cut about a 10-inch piece of tatting thread and tie it securely in a slant around the parrot's head. Cut out the eye patch, and then glue it over the thread. Glue on a gem or foam board eye. Cut a 7-inch corner off of a bandana, fold over the rough edge, and then tie it around the head. Put the hat on the head, and then sew the top of the hat to the bandana, catching the top of the head so the hat will stay in place. Flip up the back brim of the hat, and then tack it in place in the front of the head. Put the earring through the terrycloth to attach it. Tie the ribbon around the neck. Trim any snags in the material. **To make the parrot sit on a child's shoulder:** Cut a strip of Velcro® to fit under the feet. Attach one side to the feet and the other side to the shoulder of the shirt. Note: You will have to designate one shirt as the special parrot shirt!

Patterns:

Eye Patch

Trace

Eye

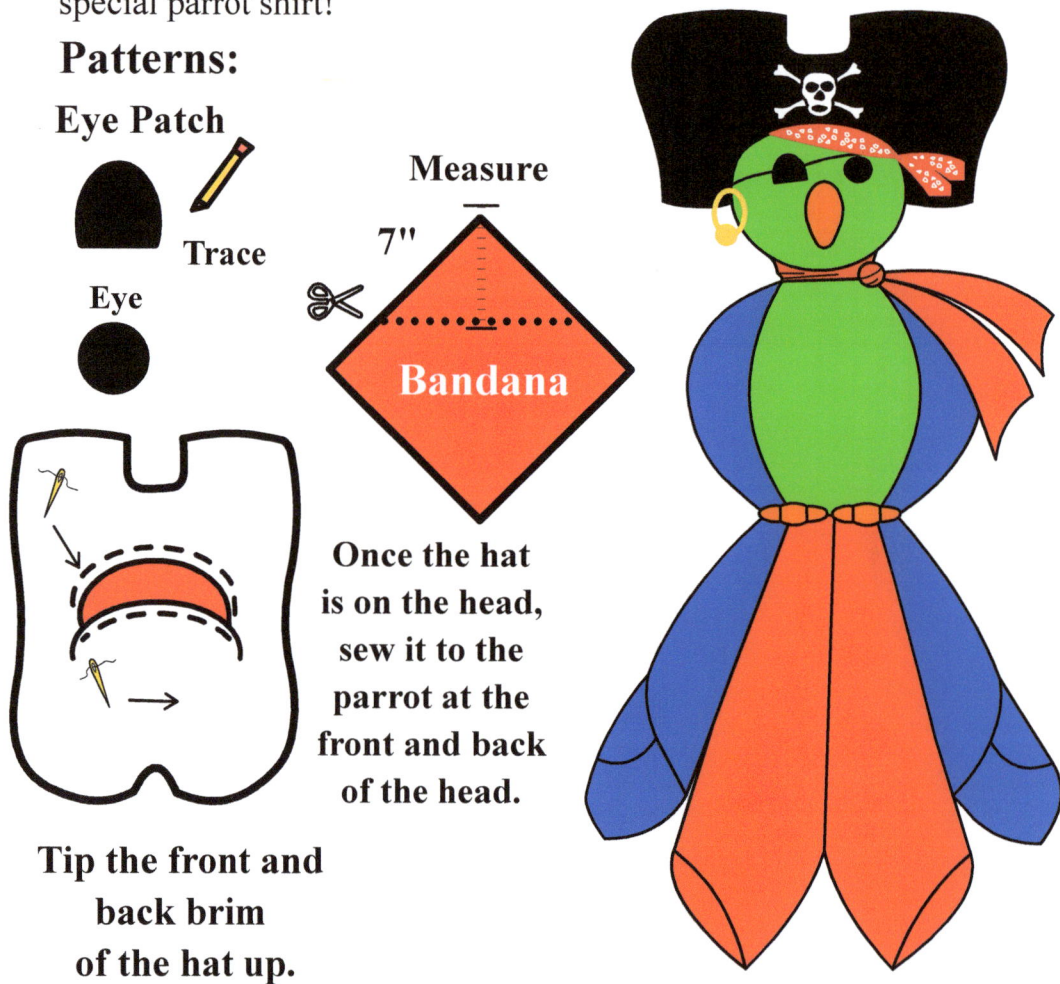

Measure 7"

Bandana

Once the hat is on the head, sew it to the parrot at the front and back of the head.

Tip the front and back brim of the hat up.

Warning: Keep sharp objects, small materials and rubber bands away from babies and small children.

Parrot Factoids

- The vocalizations of some parrots can be heard a mile away.
- Most parrots make nests in the holes of trees.
- Large parrots can live up to age 80; small parrots can live up to age 15.
- The largest parrot, the hyacinth macaw is 40 inches long and on the endangered species list.
- The smallest parrot is the pygmy parrot found in New Guinea. It is 3 1/2 inches long.
- Parrots mate for life and are monogamous.
- Parrots can bring their food to their mouths with their feet and are the only birds that can do this.
- All parrot eggs are white, no matter the variety.

TerryGami Mate's Parrot Instructions

Materials
*One green, one yellow, and one orange terrycloth washcloth approximately 12" x 12"
*One tiny black piece
*One black, 1/4" acrylic gem for the eye (a black felt patch will serve as the other eye)
*Two medium rubber bands
*One corner of a red bandana
*Red ribbon 1/2" x 6" or use a piece of bandana
*Hair clip to clip parrot on shoulder (optional)
*Needle and matching thread (green and orange)
*Tatting thread measure it so it is long enough to be tied around the head (approx. 10")
*Quilt batting or fiberfil
*Clear fabric glue (non-toxic and non-flammable)
*One gold or silver craft earring with one gold bead on it
*Scissors
*Ruler

Finished size: Approximately 12"h x 4"w.

1. Place the green cloth flat on a flat surface in a diamond shape. Roll the top corner to the center, and then roll the bottom corner to the center. Turn it over so it doesn't unroll.

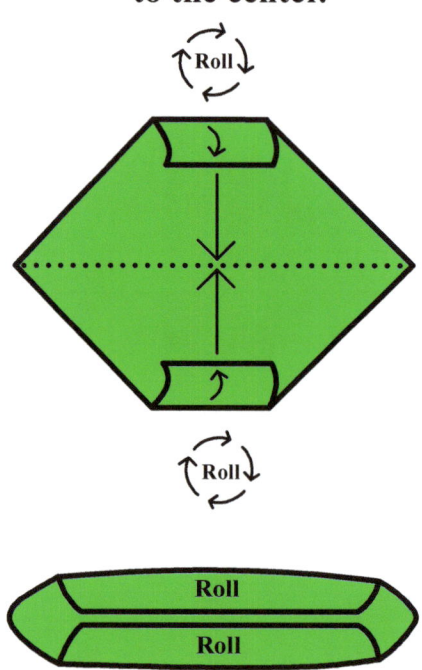

Roll opposite corners to the center.

Continue...

TerryGami Mate's Parrot Instructions

2. **A)** Place the yellow cloth flat on a flat surface in a diamond shape. Measure up 4 inches from the bottom corner of the cloth. **B)** Roll that bottom corner up to the 4-inch mark. **C)** Roll the top corner down to meet the bottom roll. Turn the cloth over so it doesn't unroll.

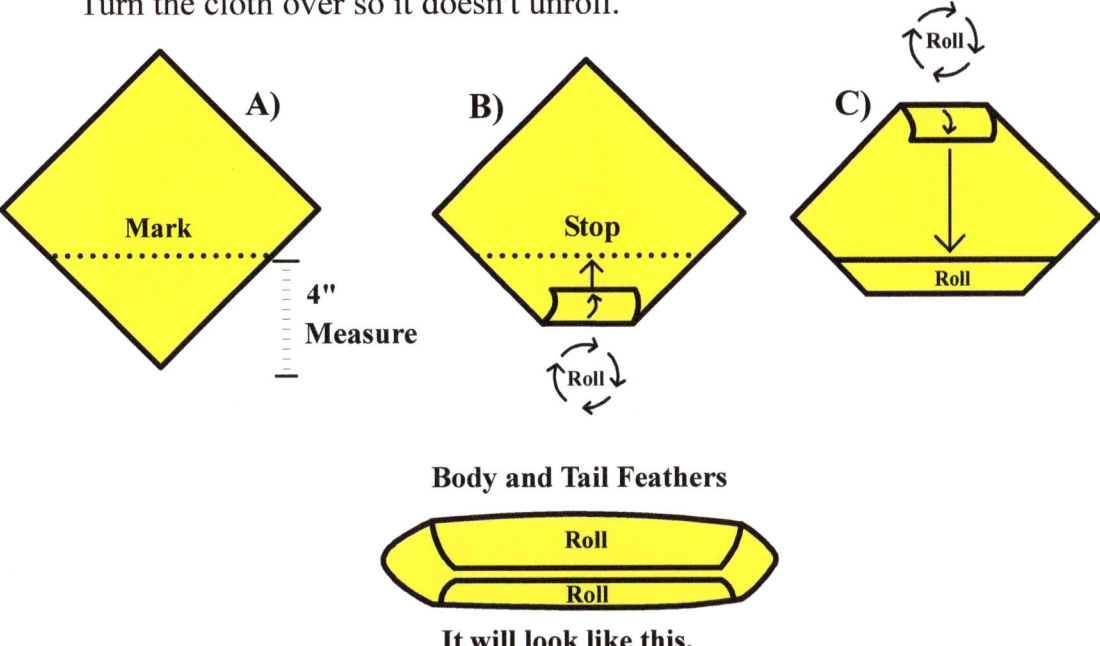

3. **To make the head piece: A)** With the rolls of the cloth on the inside, fold the green cloth in half, making sure the corners are even. **B)** Measure down 2 inches from the fold, and then **C)** wrap a rubber band.

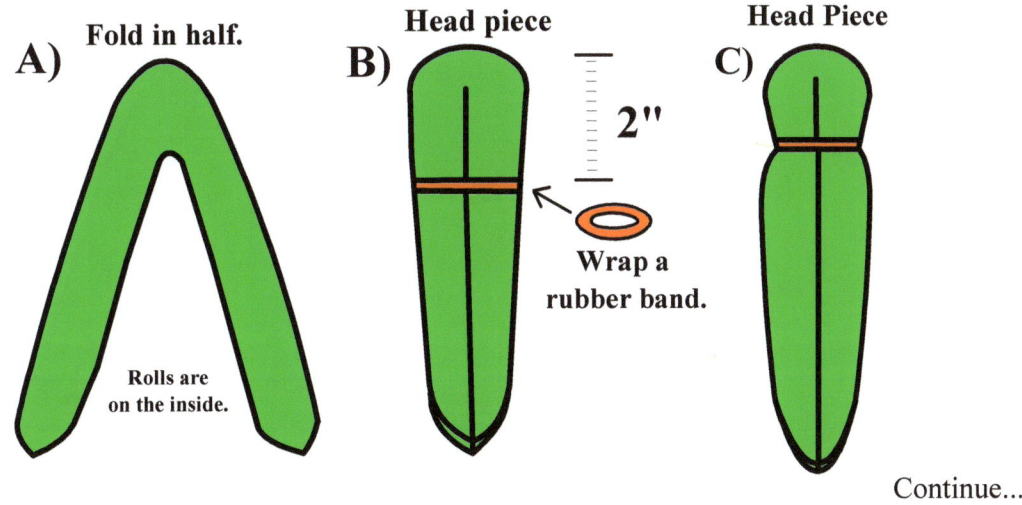

Continue...

TerryGami Captain's Parrot Instructions

4. **A)** Stuff and round out the head piece. **B)** Open up the bottom corners.

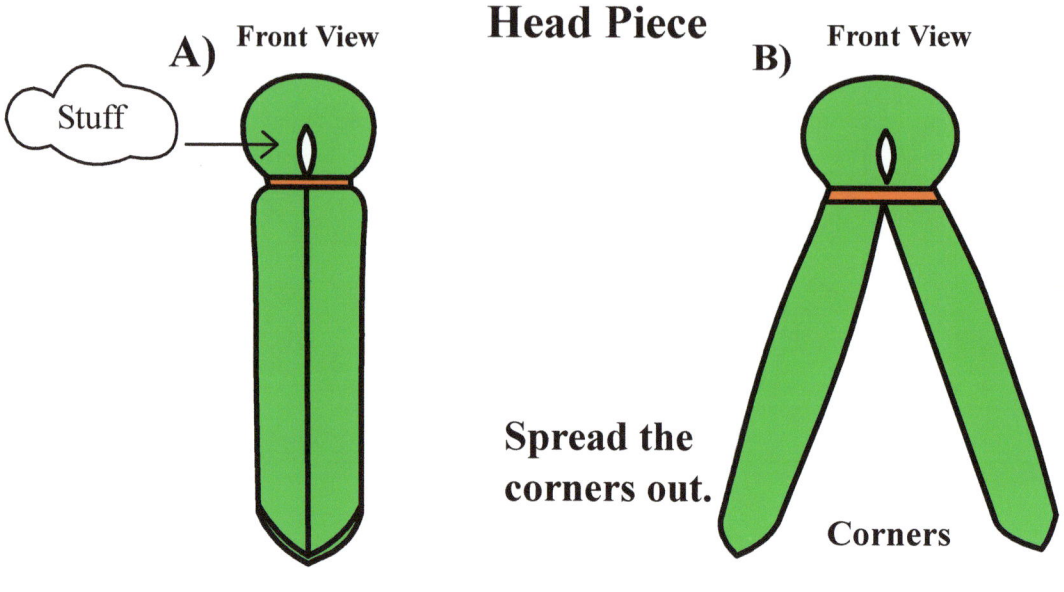

5. **A)** Fold the yellow cloth in half with the rolls on the inside, making sure the ends are even. **B)** Place the head piece over the fold of the yellow body piece.

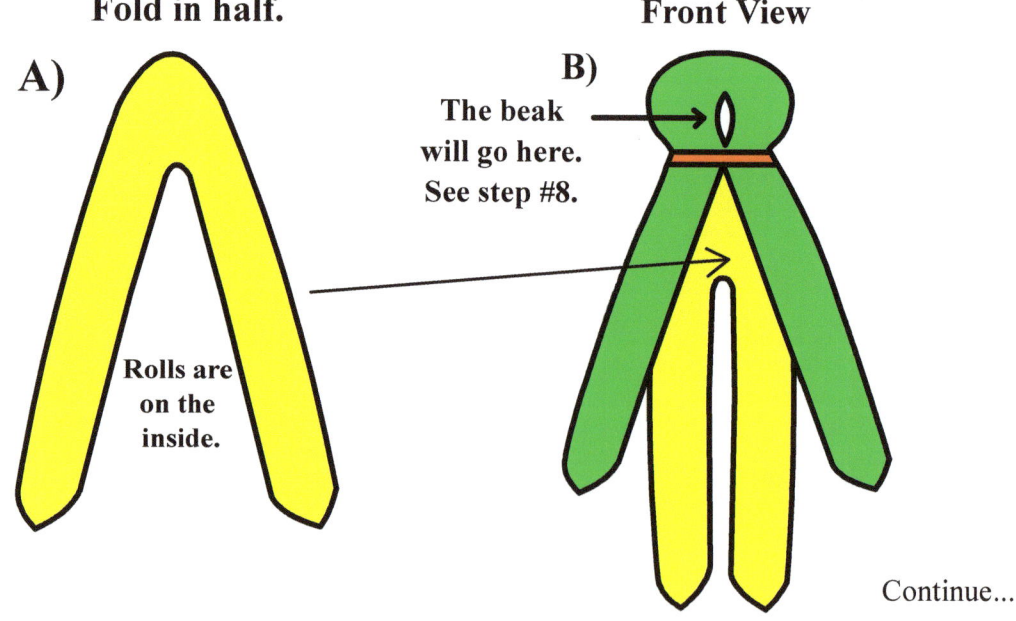

Continue...

TerryGami Mate's Parrot Instructions

6. Curve the body of the bird toward the back. The entire fold of the yellow washcloth will be the bird's chest. Make sure both ends of the green and yellow tail ends are even. Wrap a rubber band two inches up from the green tail end.

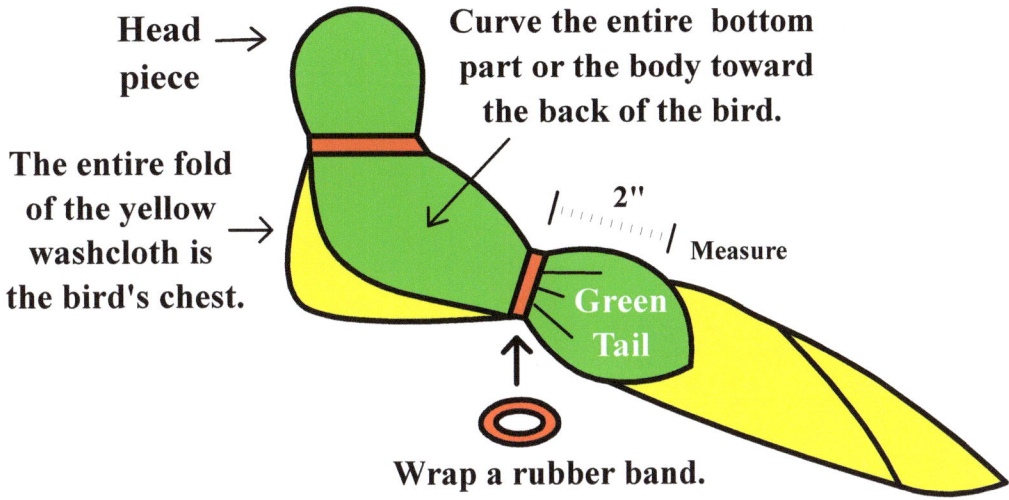

7. Using a whip stitch, cover the rubber bands with the material around the rubber band (optional). Note: Fancy rubber bands can be used or cover rubber bands with ribbon or yarn.

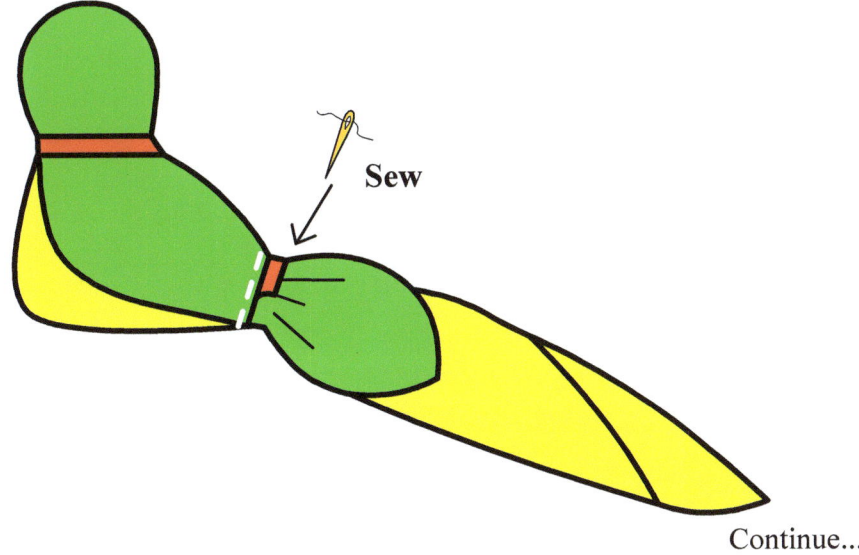

Continue...

TerryGami Mate's Parrot Instructions

8. **To make the beak**: A) Measure down 1 1/2 inches from one of the corners on the orange cloth, mark it, and then cut the corner off. B) Cut about 1/4 inch off each side of the corner. C) Fold over the rough edge about 1/2 inch, D) and then roll each side to the middle. E) Sew or glue the rolls together, tapering the beak at the corner end. F) Turn over, and then sew or glue the beak to the face about 1 1/4 inch from the top of the head. Sew down the end of the beak so it curves a bit.

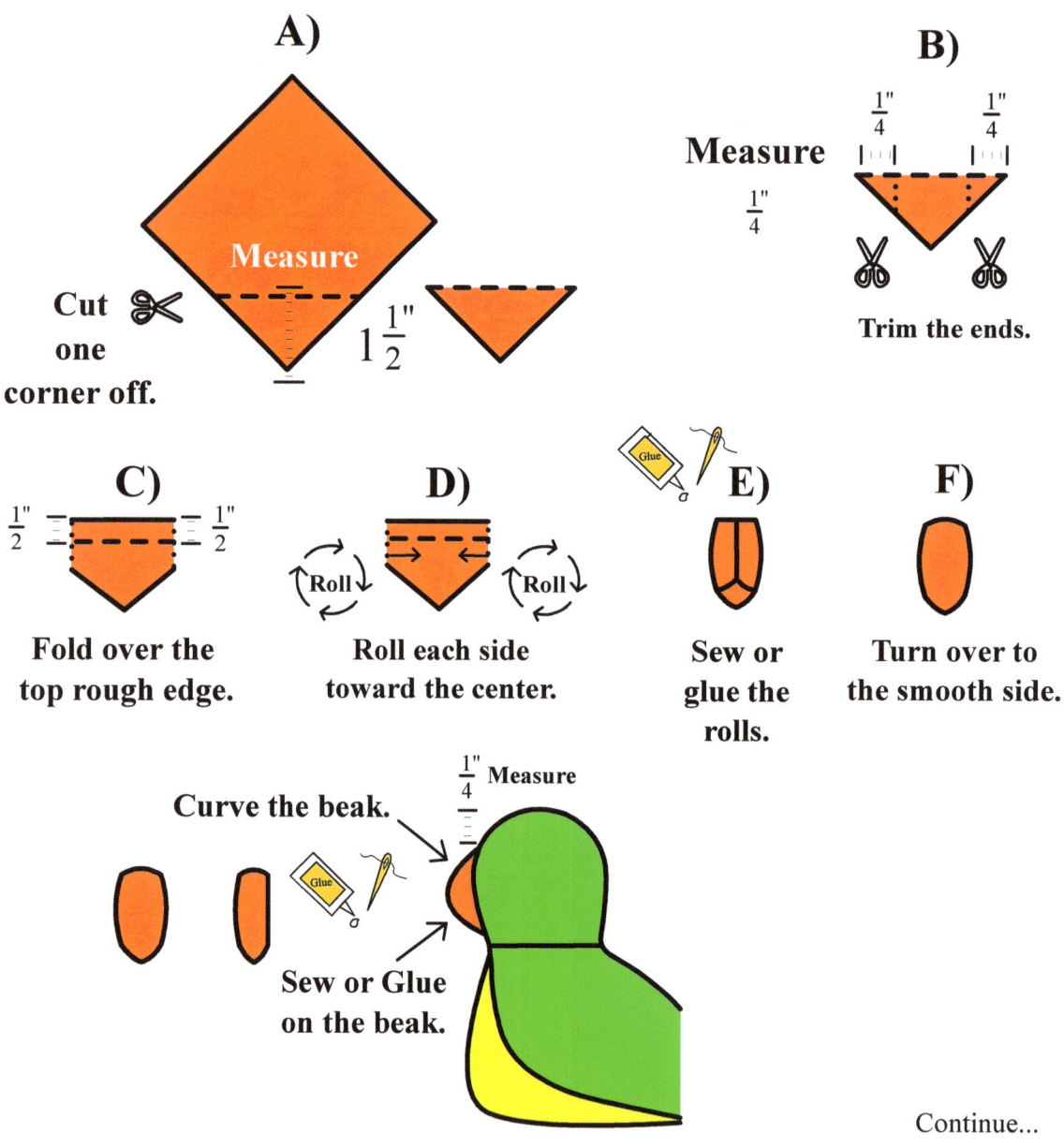

Continue...

TerryGami Mate's Parrot Instructions

9. **To make the feet:** **A)** Place the orange cloth flat on a flat surface. Measure down about 1 1/2 inch from two of the corners, mark them off, and then cut the corner off. **B)** Fold the side corners over so the piece measures about 3/4 of an inch, and then **C)** roll the rough edges to the end of the corner. Trim to fit the parrot, if necessary.

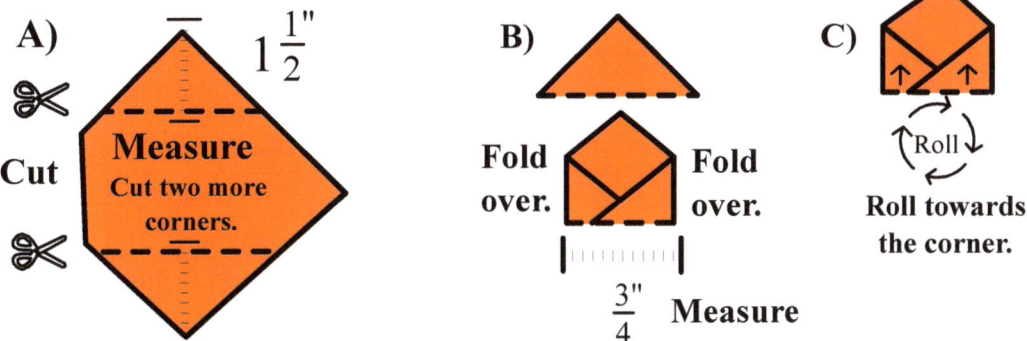

Using the whip stitch, sew the edges together, but as you sew and reach the first 1/4-inch mark, wrap the thread around the entire piece creating a toe. Sew another 1/4 inch, and then wrap the thread around the piece at this point, creating the last two toes. Sew the seam side of the piece to one side of the green corner which extends below the rubber band, leaving enough room for the other foot. Repeat this step for the second foot, and then attach it.

Note: If you want he foot to curve a bit, sew a running stitch through the entire length of the back and pull the thread tight, and then tie off the thread.

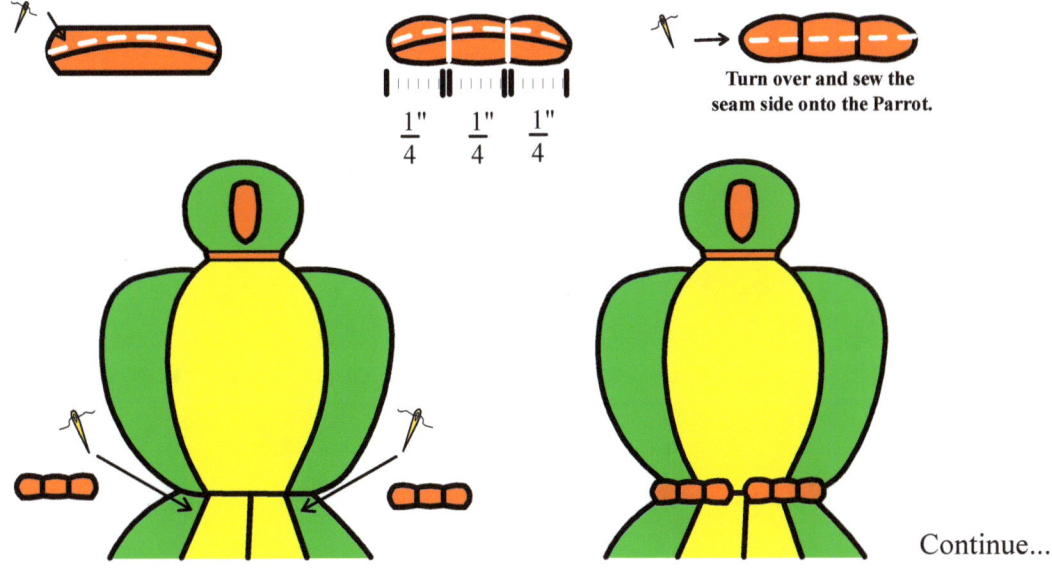

Continue...

10. TerryGami Captain's Parrot Instructions

Cut about a 10-inch piece of tatting thread and tie it securely in a slant around the parrot's head. Cut out the eye patch, and then glue it over the thread. Glue on a gem or foam board eye. Cut a 7-inch corner off of a bandana, fold over the rough edge, and then tie it around the head. Put the earring through the terrycloth to attach it. Tie the ribbon around the neck. Trim any snags. **To attach the parrot to your shoulder:** Cut two strips of Velcro®. Attach the soft side of the Velcro under the parrot's feet. Attach the rough side of the Velcro to the shoulder of the shirt. Attach the parrot to the shirt with the Velcro®.

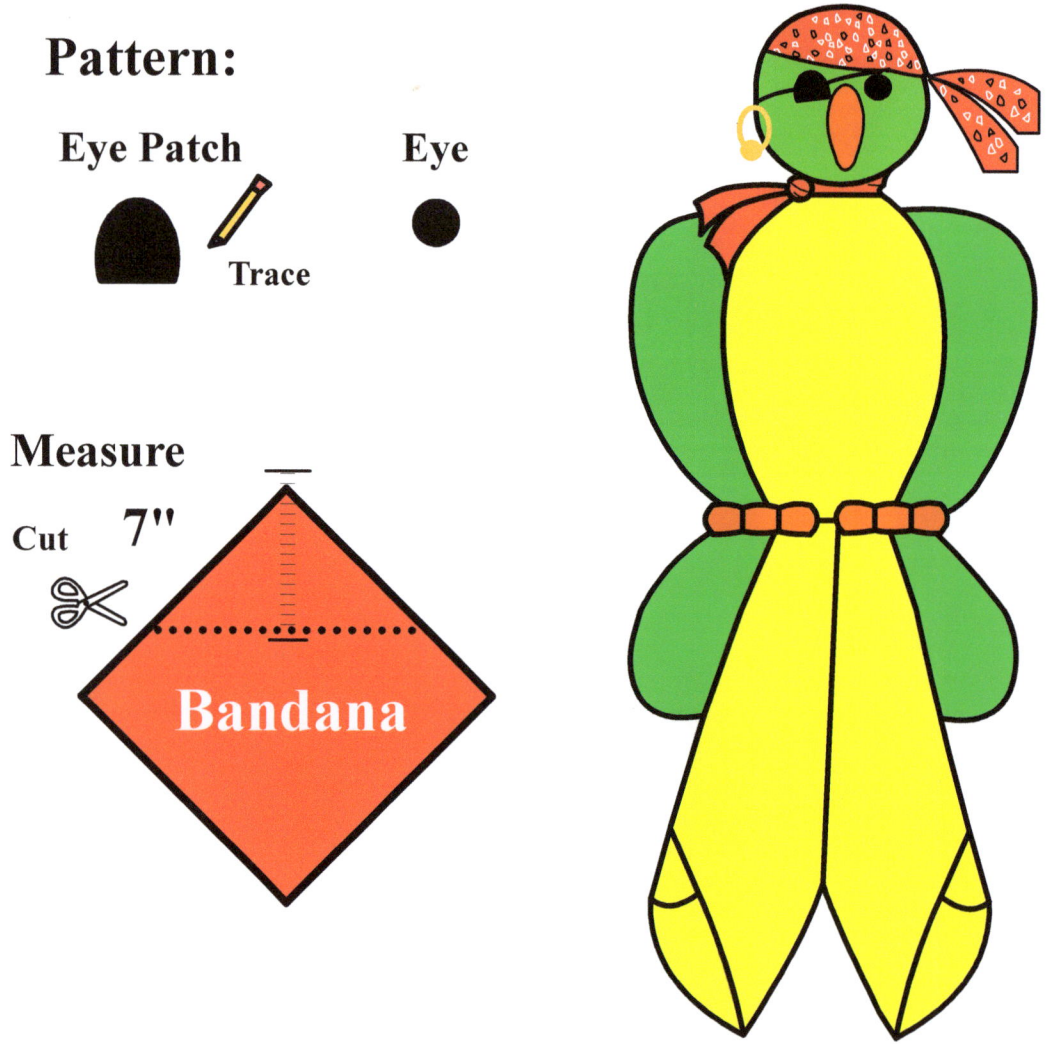

Pattern:

Eye Patch **Eye**

Trace

Measure

Cut 7"

Bandana

Warning: Keep sharp objects, small materials and rubber bands away from babies and small children.

Mushroom Factoids

- A mushroom is a spore-bearing fungi that feeds either on soil, debris or other organisms.
- The living body or the mycelium of the mushroom is hidden underground and consists of tiny filaments which can be very tiny or cover acres.
- The fleshy part of the mushroom we see above ground is the "fruit" of the fungi.
- There are about two million species of fungi on the earth, but only about 80,000 have been identified.
- Mushrooms are more closely related to animals than plants because they "inhale" oxygen and "exhale" carbon dioxide. Their proteins are similar to animal proteins.
- Mushrooms grow from spores rather than seed.
- The spores are protected from the elements by the mushroom's cap. One mushroom can have billions of spores.

TerryGami Mushroom Instructions

Materials
*One thin, orange terrycloth washcloth approximately 12" x 12"
*Two thin, cream terrycloth washcloths approximately 12" x 12" (See the note below.)
*Clear fabric glue (non-toxic and non-flammable)
*Cream and orange thread
*Needle
*Quilt batting or fiber fill
*Two medium rubber bands
*Pencil and tracing paper or thin paper
*Scissors
*Ruler

Note: If you are using felt, foam board or gems for the spots, you will only need one cream washcloth.

Finished size: Approximately 4" x 4"

1. Place the cream cloth flat on a flat surface in a diamond shape. Roll the top and bottom corners to the center of the cloth.

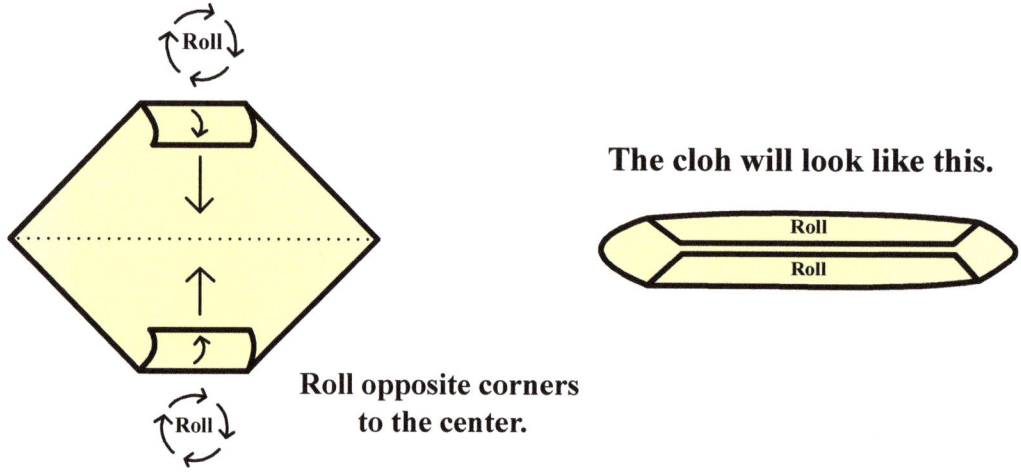

The cloh will look like this.

Roll opposite corners to the center.

2. Fold the cloth in half with the rolls on the inside, and then measure down 5 inches from the corners and wrap a rubber band.

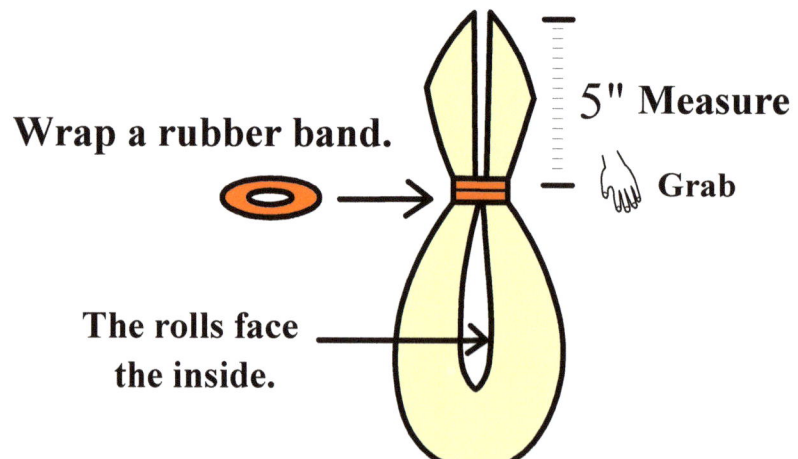

Continue...

TerryGami Mushroom Instructions

3. Turn the piece to the smooth side of the stem. Unroll the corners, and then spread them all the way out. Curn the corner down around the stem, making a tube on each side.

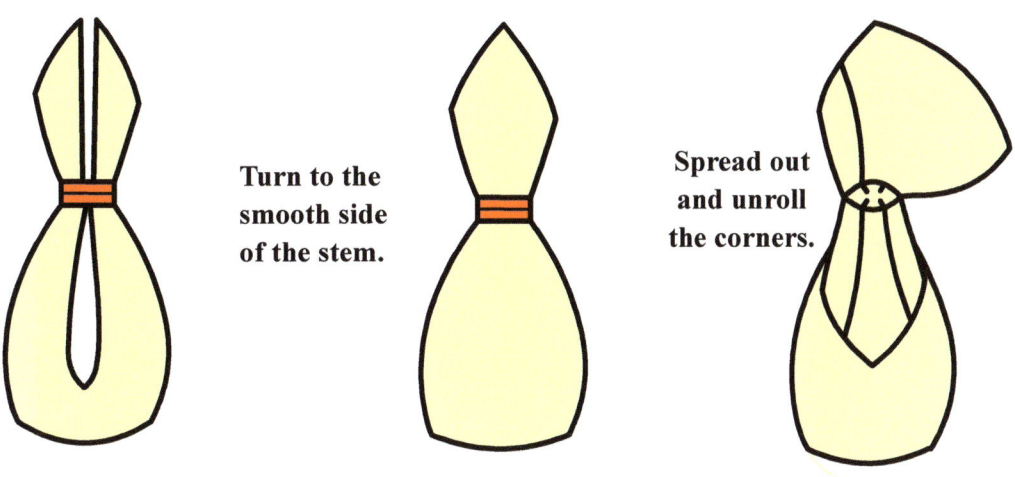

Turn to the smooth side of the stem.

Spread out and unroll the corners.

4. Gather the piece around the top of the stem, hold it in place, and then wrap a rubber band, leaving one inch of the corners below the rubber band on each side. Stuff the top of the mushroom with batting. Sew the edges together on each side of the mushroom, forming a tube all around and making sure the mushroom top is as round as possible before you sew.

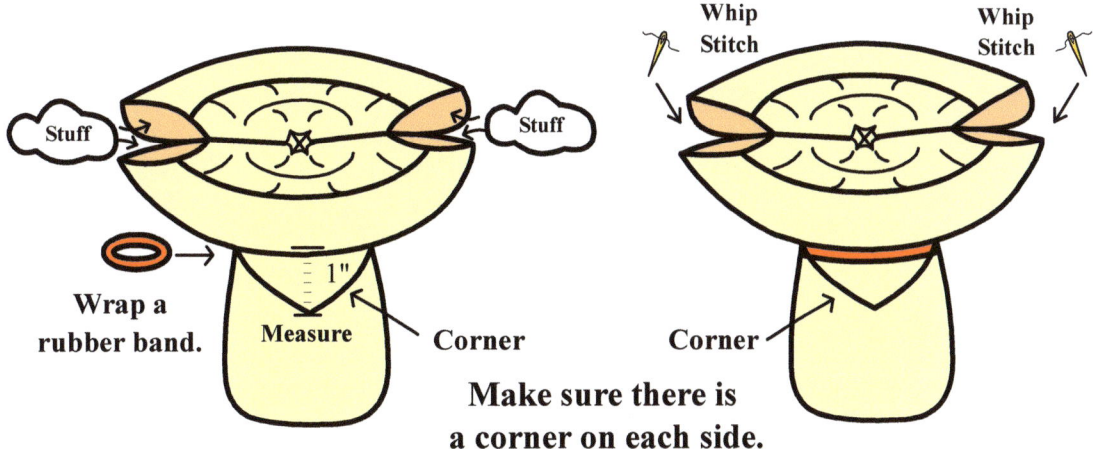

Stuff

Wrap a rubber band.

Measure

Corner

Whip Stitch

Whip Stitch

Corner

Make sure there is a corner on each side.

Continue...

TerryGami Mushroom Instructions

5. Fill the top of the mushroom with batting, making sure to round out the mound of stuffing as much as possible.

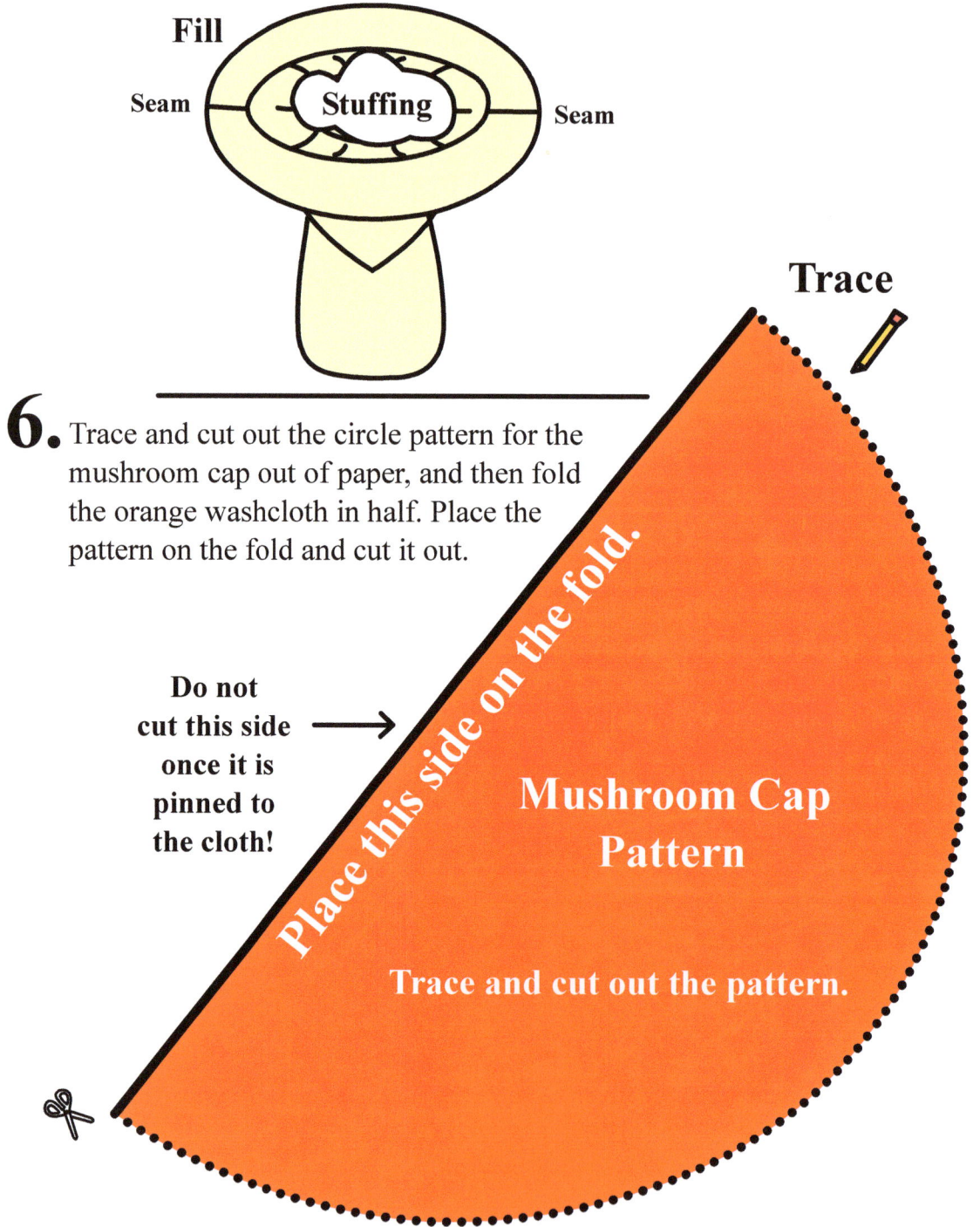

6. Trace and cut out the circle pattern for the mushroom cap out of paper, and then fold the orange washcloth in half. Place the pattern on the fold and cut it out.

Do not cut this side once it is pinned to the cloth!

Place this side on the fold.

Mushroom Cap Pattern

Trace and cut out the pattern.

Continue...

TerryGami Mushroom Instructions

7. Sew a running stitch 1/4 inch from the edge around the entire circle. When you get to the end, pull the thread slightly so it will gather the material so the edges can be turned under, and also so the circle will fit the top of the mushroom. Place the circle on top of the mushroom. The gather will help you to turn the edge under 1/4 inch or more, if necessary. Use double thread. See page on sewing by hand. Stuff the mushroom.

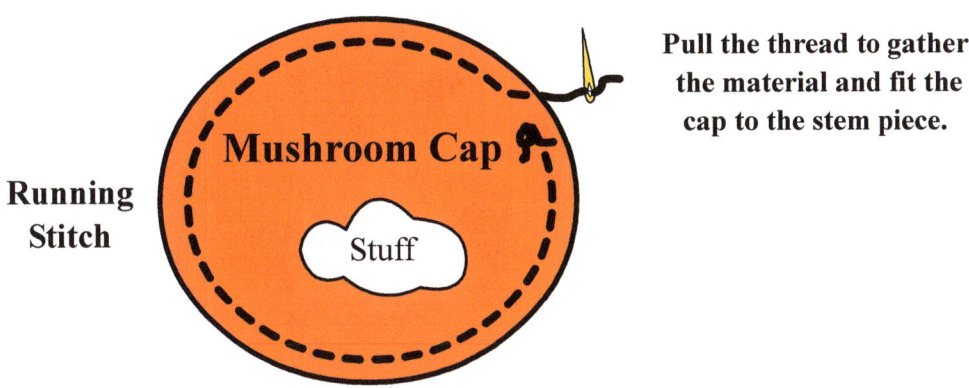

8. Fold the edge under 1/4 inch, more or less, and then sew or glue the mushroom cap to the stem piece, making sure to adjust and manipulate the stuffing into a round shape, as you work. Also, make sure a little of the top cream part of the mushroom shows, when viewed from the side. See step number 9.

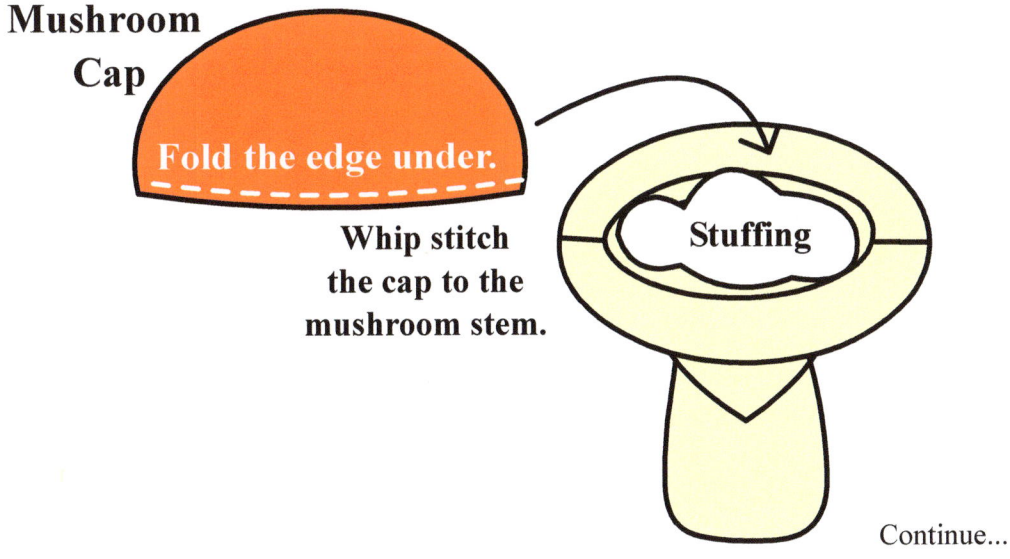

Continue...

TerryGami Mushroom Instructions

9. Sew or glue around the base of the mushroom top to cover the rubber band. Turn to the side and sew or glue the hole in the stem on each side, unless you want to use it as a Boo Boo Mushroom or as a party favor to hold a treat. The flaps on the underside can be shaped, stuffed, and sewn as desired. Hint: Flaps may be turned into arms.

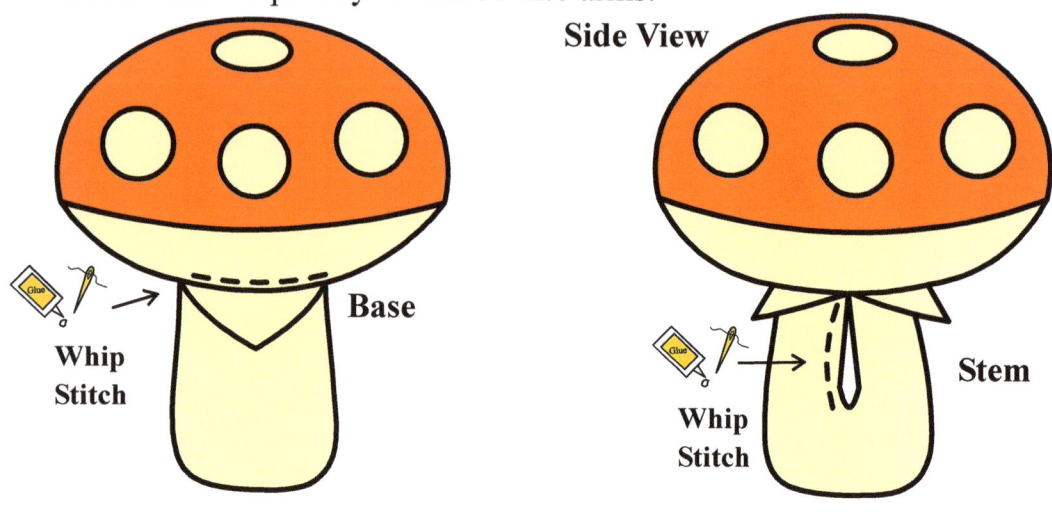

10. Trace the pattern and cut out about seven circles from the second cream washcloth (or from felt or form board, or use large gems). Glue them to the cap of the mushroom. Trim any snags.

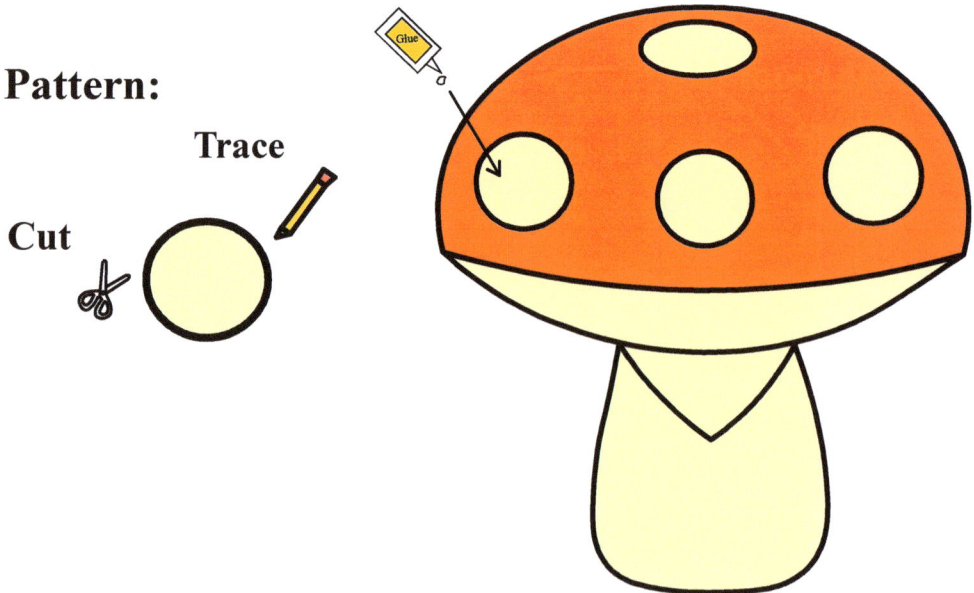

Warning: Keep sharp objects, small materials and rubber bands away from babies and small children.

Gnome Factoids

According to legend:

- Gnomes are said to bear only twins; one girl and one boy.

- A gnome pregnancy lasts for 12 months.

- Gnomes are born under a tree, which then becomes their birthday tree.

- Gnomes will either build their homes under their birth tree or visit the tree every year on their birthdays.

- Gnomes are said to be smarter than men and can communicate by telepathy.

- Gnomes rarely marry until they are 200 years old.

- Gnomes can live up to 400 years.

TerryGami Baby Gnome Instructions

Materials:
*Two pink and one peach, thin terrycloth washcloth approximately 12" x 12"
*Two medium sized rubber bands
*White ribbon 1/8" x 12"
*Small piece of white foam board to make the hearts or pre-cut hearts
*White baby terry yarn 10" piece for hair or regular white yarn
*Black tatting thread 1" piece
*One jingle bell 1/4 inch
*Clear fabric glue (non-toxic and non-flammable)
*Needle (blunt-end, optional)
*Matching thread
*Heart hole punch 1/4" or pre-cut foam board pieces
*Quilt batting or stuffing
*Scissors
*Ruler

Finished size: Approximately 7"h x 5"w.

1. Place one of the pink cloths flat on a flat surface in a diamond shape. Roll the opposite corners to the center of the cloth.

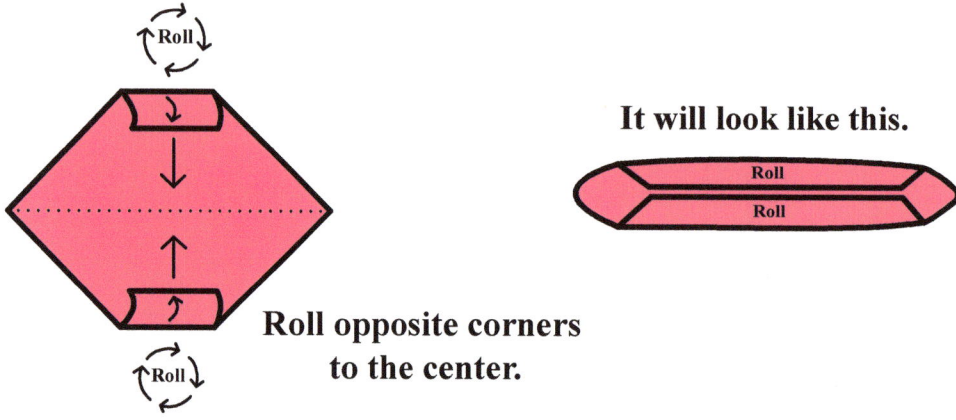

It will look like this.

Roll opposite corners to the center.

---

2. Fold the cloth in half with the rolls on the outside, and then measure down 4 inches from the corners and wrap a rubber band.

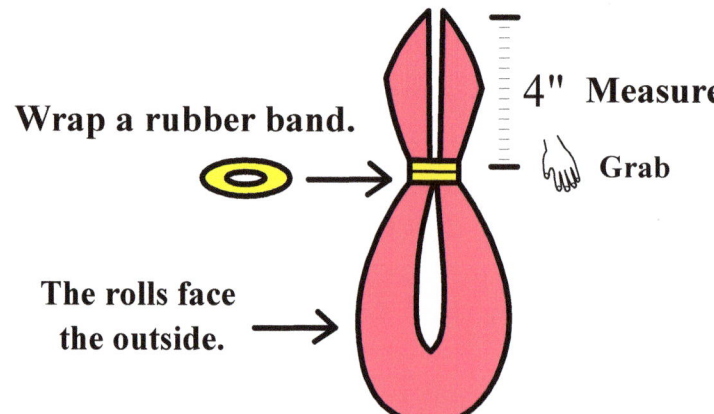

Wrap a rubber band.

4" Measure

Grab

The rolls face the outside.

Continue...

TerryGami Baby Gnome Instructions

3. Turn the cloth inside out so that the rolls and the corners are on the inside of the cloth.

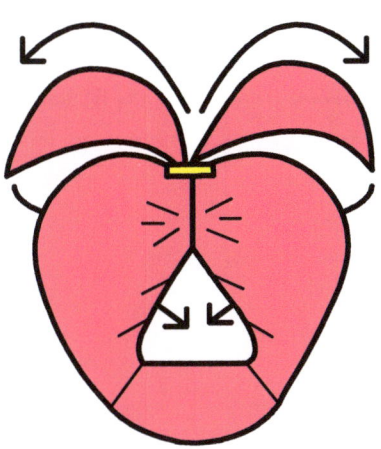

Turn the cloth inside out.

The rolls will now face the inside.

It will look like this.

---

4. Pull the corners out, one on each side. To make the bottom of the Gnome somewhat pointed, tighten the rolls together at the bottom, and then sew the rolls together. It will be a bit tricky because the rolls are on the inside.

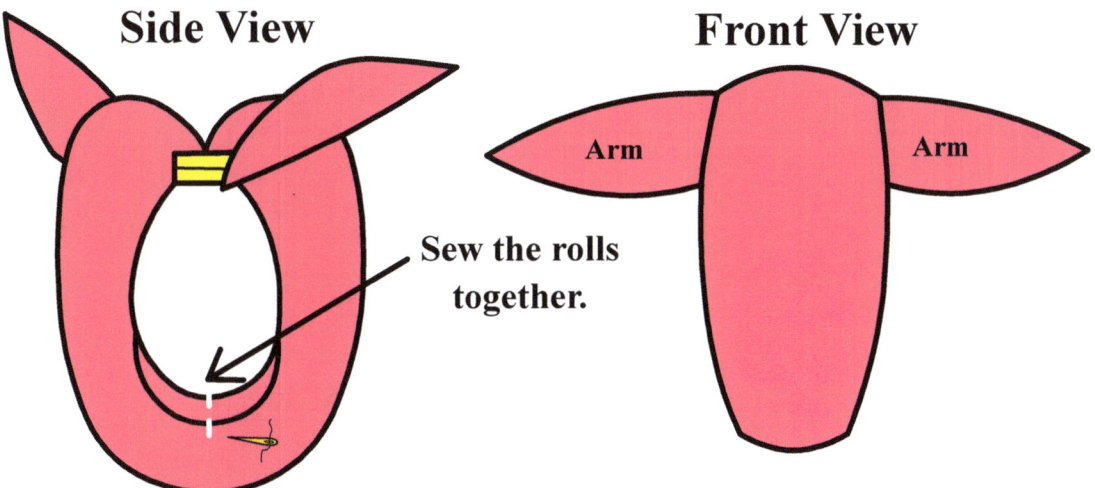

Continue...

75

TerryGami Baby Gnome Instructions

5. **A)** Cut the peach cloth in half. **B)** Roll the longest sides to the center of the cloth.

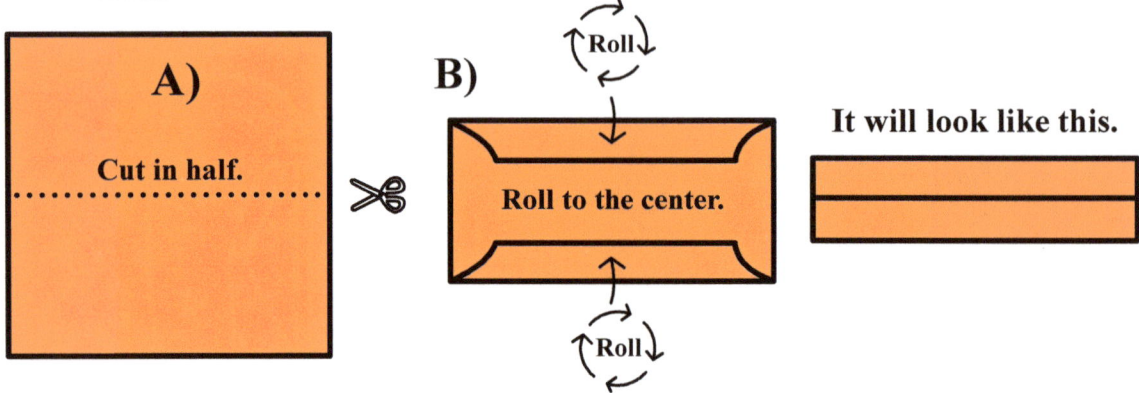

6. To form the head: **A)** Fold the cloth in half with the rolls on the inside. **B)** Measure down 1 1/2 inch from the fold, and then wrap a rubber band. **C)** Stuff the head. **D)** Turn the cloth so the smooth side faces towards you.

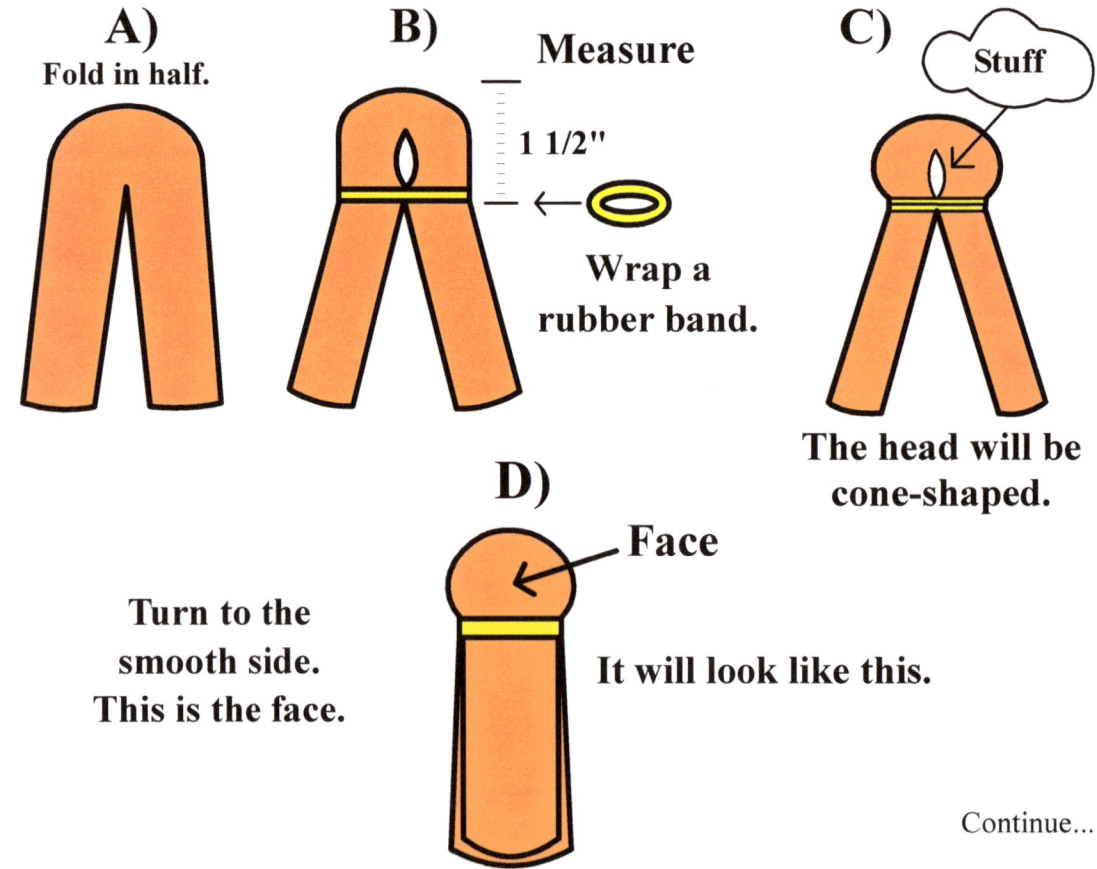

Continue...

TerryGami Baby Gnome Instructions

7. **To make the head**: pull the bottom of the head piece between the rubber bands at the top of the body piece. Make sure the rubber band on the neck is fully covered by the top of the body.

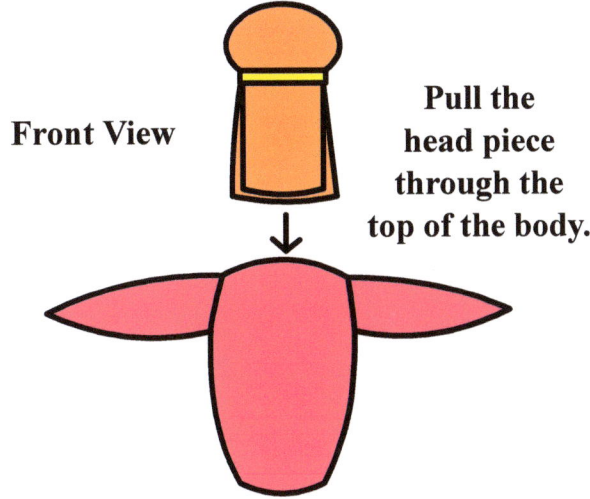

8. **To make the arms:** Pull out the ends of the peach cloth on each side, and then tuck the ends into the pink corners. The peach ends will act as the stuffing for the arms. If there is too much material from the peach cloth, trim it to fit inside of the pink cloth. Fold over the ends of the pink corners so the arms measure 1 1/2 inches, and then re-roll the sides of the arms to the center. Sew (whip stitch) the seams of the arms closed. Twist the arms so the seams face downwards.

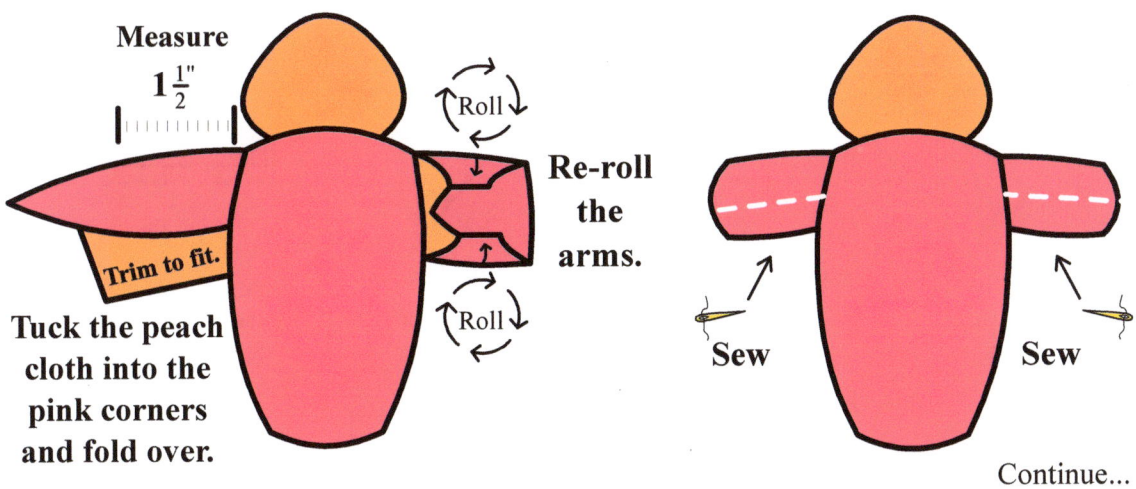

Continue...

77

TerryGami Baby Gnome Instructions

9. **To make the hair:** Loop the yarn into three loops, and then sew the yarn onto the head.

10. A) Measure down 3 1/2 inches from the corner of the second pink cloth, then mark it. Cut off the corner to make a triangle. Make sure it will fit before you sew it because the head size will vary due to the size of the cloth and how tightly the rolls were rolled on the head piece. Trim to fit, if necessary. Sew (whip stitch) a 1/4-inch hem at the bottom of the hat.
B) Fold it in half with the hem seam on the outside, and then sew the side of the hat closed. Sew a piece of pipe cleaner inside of the hat on the seam, if you want the hat to bend, but make sure you fold over the ends of the pipe cleaner so the sharp ends won't poke out.

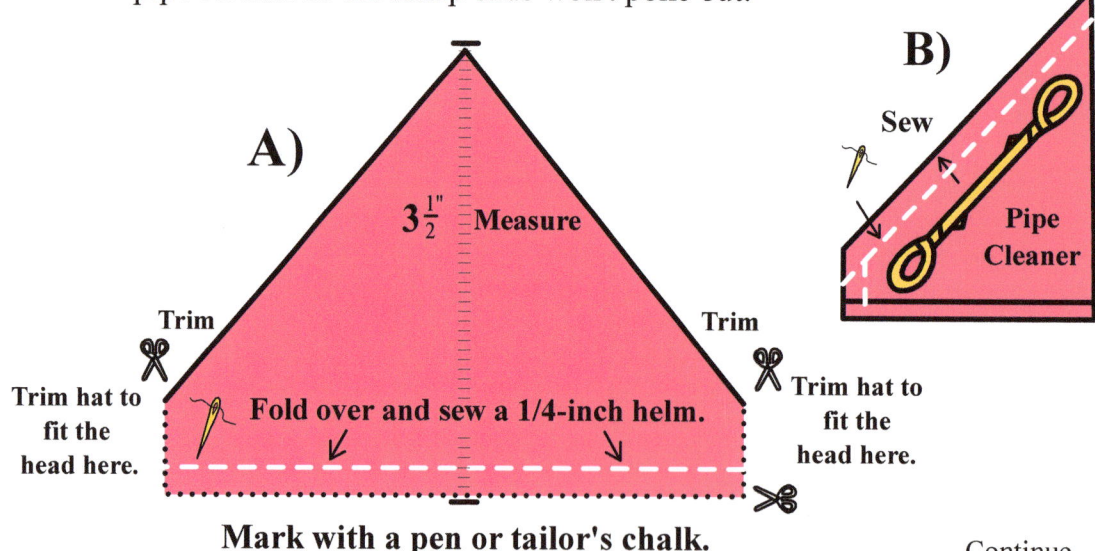

Continue...

TerryGami Baby Gnome Instructions

11. Sew on the jingle bell to the top of the hat. Sew the hat to the head.

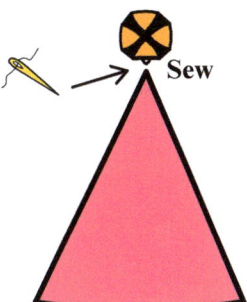

12. Tie a bow around the neck. Glue on the 1/4-inch, black tatting thread to form the eyes. Glue on the hearts to the hat and body. Sew (whip stitch) the sides closed, if you are not making a Boo Boo Gnome. Trim any snags. Make a blue Baby Gnome to complete the set of Gnome twins.

Sew the sides closed, if not making a Boo Boo Gnome.

Leave the sides open, if making a Boo Boo Gnome.

To make a Baby Boo Boo Gnome, attach this card.

Baby Boo Boo Gnome
"When a boo boo has you feeling crummy,
tuck an ice cube in my tummy.
Hold it to your boo boo tight,
and soon it will feel all right!"

Warning: Keep sharp objects, small materials and rubber bands away from babies and small children.

Gnome Factoids

- In German and Scandinavian folklore, a gnome is a diminutive, earth spirit that is said to bring good fortune and good luck to households.
- Some gnomes are said to guard mines and underground treasures.
- Gnome enemies are trolls, unkind humans and anyone who harms the environment.
- Gnomes are pranksters and love practical jokes.
- In the evening, male gnomes like to sit on toadstools and smoke their pipes.
- Gnomes are said to have the strength of seven men.

TerryGami Gnome Instructions

Materials:
*One turquoise, two peach, and two green, thin terrycloth washcloths, approximately 12" x12"
*One brown felt square for shoes and belt
*Small piece of dark brown foam board or felt for eyes
*One half of a red felt square for hat
*Small piece of red foam board or felt for mouth
*Small piece of gold or yellow felt or foam board for the belt buckle
*Sewing needles, regular for felt and blunt-end for terrycloth (optional)
*Red, turquoise, green and brown thread
*Feather (optional)
*Three medium rubber bands, plus a few extra
*Clear fabric craft glue (non-toxic and non-flammable)
*Small bunch of pink and white silk flowers
*Stick 8" or 9" long for a walking stick
*Six to eight large pipe cleaners (optional)
*Hole punch (1/4") for eyes and mouth
*Small pebbles or small rocks for the pedestal base
*Chop stick or a 12" stick to help the gnome stand
*Two 1/2" pieces of velcro to attach the feet to the pedestal
*Quilt batting
*Scissors
*Ruler

> **Note:** To make a young boy gnome, modify the hair in Step #17 of the girl gnome instructions. Cut the yarn five or six inches a piece, or cut the yarn to the desired length by measuring it against the gnome.

Finished size: Approximately 13"h x 7" w.

1. Cut the tags off of all of the cloths. Place one peach washcloth flat on a flat surface in a diamond shape. Roll the opposite corners to the center of the cloth. Repeat with the green cloth, but if making a standing gnome, add the pipe cleaners. Turn the cloths over so they won't unroll. In order to stand, the gnome will require a pedestal. (See steps 16 and 17.)

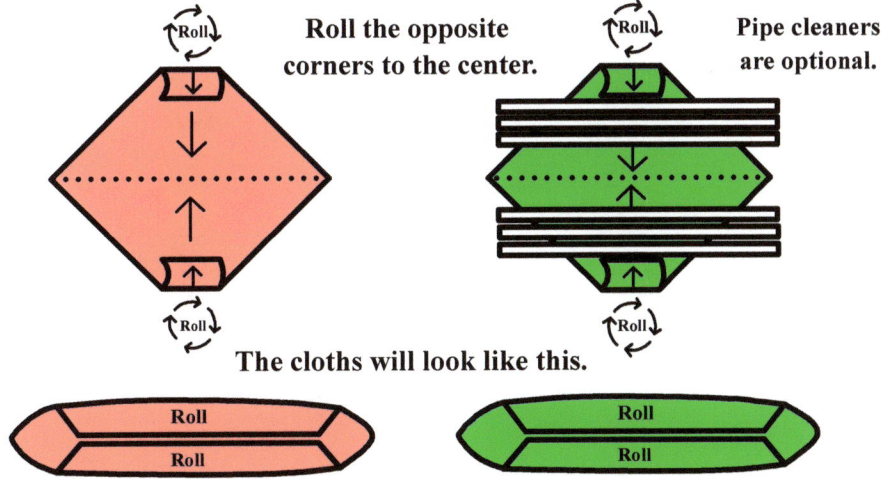

Roll the opposite corners to the center.   Pipe cleaners are optional.

The cloths will look like this.

The peach cloth will be half of the body.   The green cloth will be the legs.   Continue...

TerryGami Gnome Instructions

2. **A)** Place the second peach cloth on a flat surface in a diamond shape. **B)** Fold the top and bottom corners so that the corners meet in the center. **C)** Turn the cloth over, holding the corners in place. Pin or lightly tape in place, if necessary. **D)** Roll the folded sides to the center. The corners will flip up. **E)** The cloth will look like this. This cloth will be part of the body. The center corners will become the ears. Turn the cloth over so it doesn't unroll.

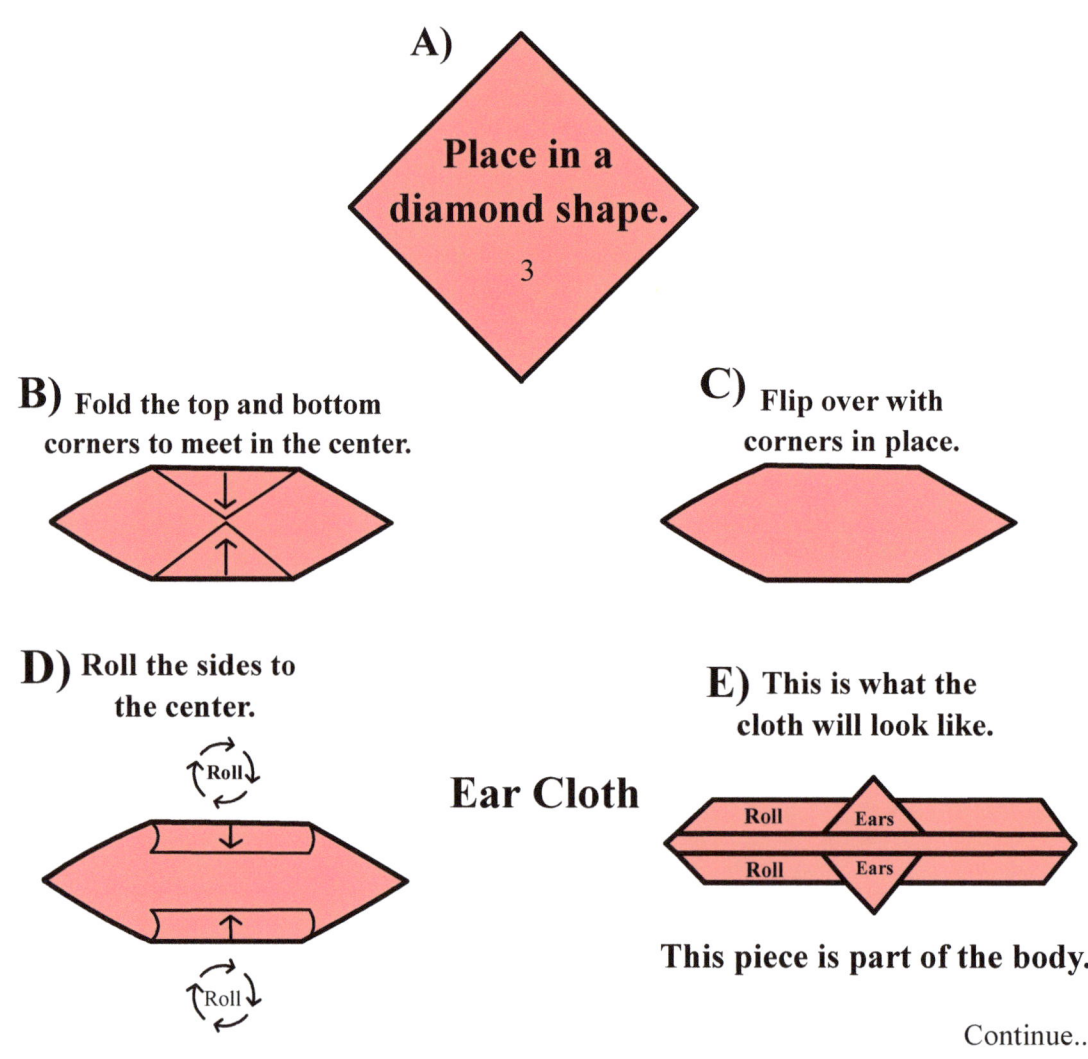

A) Place in a diamond shape.

B) Fold the top and bottom corners to meet in the center.

C) Flip over with corners in place.

D) Roll the sides to the center.

E) This is what the cloth will look like.

Ear Cloth

This piece is part of the body.

Continue...

TerryGami Gnome Instructions

3. Stack the two peach cloths. The ear cloth should be on the bottom with the rolls facing down and the other cloth should be on top with the rolls facing up.

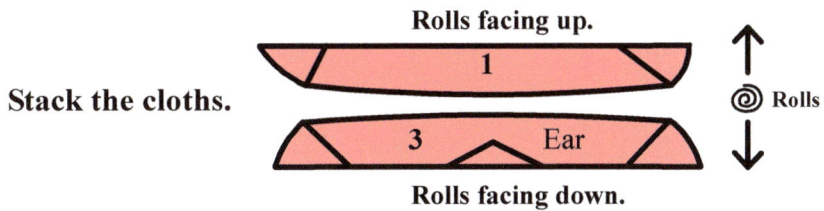

4. Measure down 4 inches from the corners on the left end, and then wrap a rubber band. Measure down 5 inches from the corners on the other end, and then wrap a rubber band.

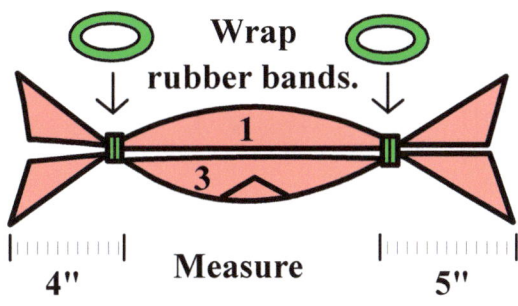

5. Now turn the ensemble inside out so that all of the corners are on the inside, including the corners that will become the ears.

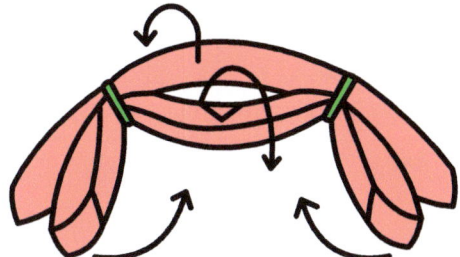
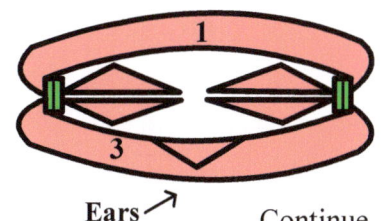

Continue...

TerryGami Gnome Instructions

6. **A)** Turn the ensemble upright, and then **B)** pull out the top 5-inch corners, one on each side. They will be the arms. The bottom corners remain tucked inside of the body.

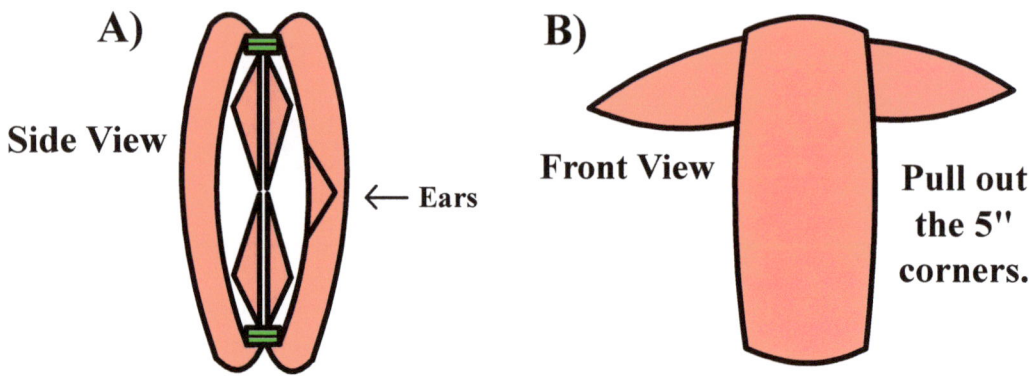

7. **To form the head and ears: A)** Roll the side with the ears up above the rubber band. **B)** Measure down two 2 inches from the top. Wrap a rubber band at this point, making sure the ears are above the rubber band.

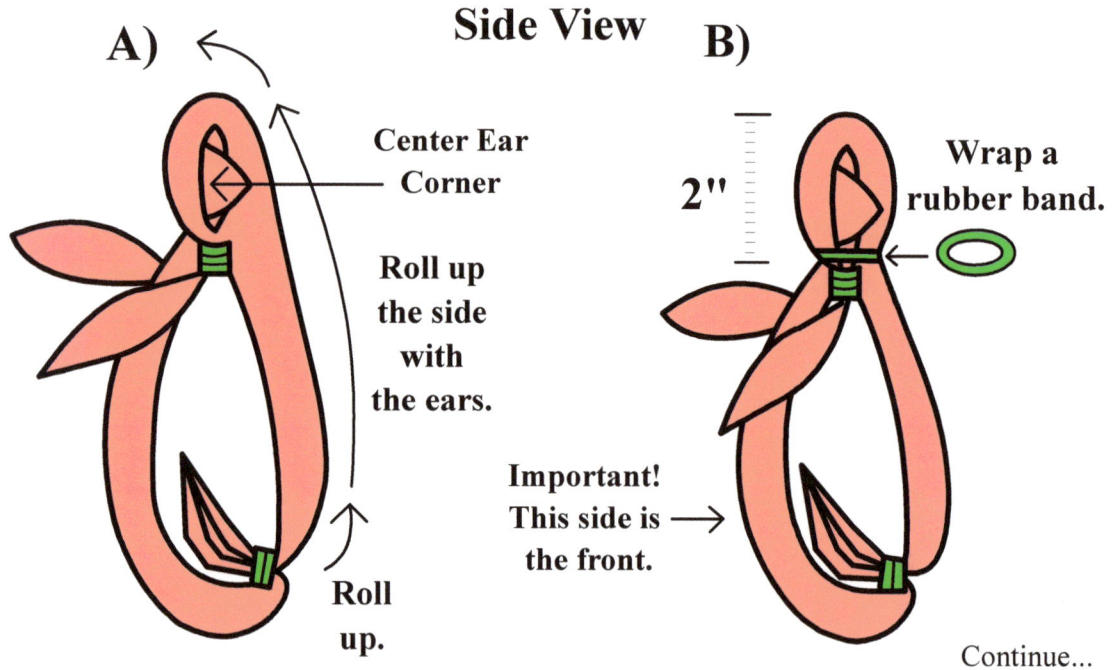

Continue...

TerryGami Gnome Instructions

8. **To form the legs:** Pull the green, rolled cloth through the bottom of the body, making sure the corners are even and that the rolls are facing down. Re-roll the arms and legs, if necessary. Stuff the arms and legs with strips of quilt batting.

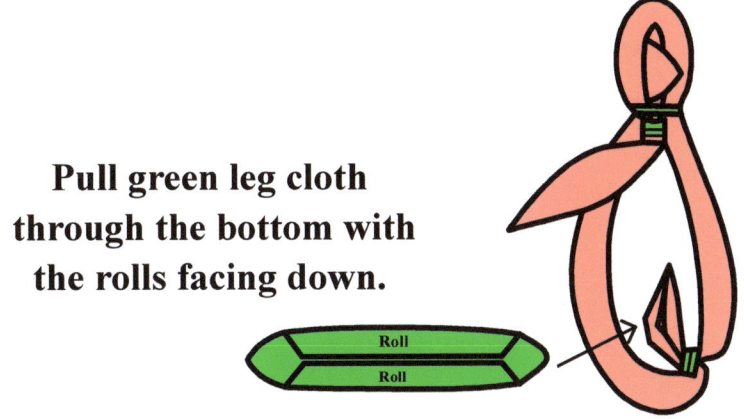

Pull green leg cloth through the bottom with the rolls facing down.

9. **Stuff the body and head:** Separate the rolls slightly inside of the head and stomach, leaving the bottom corners tucked inside. Shape the ears into points, tucking the excess material into the head. Add stuffing to the head and the stomach. Shape and straighten the back, bringing the shoulders together above the arms.

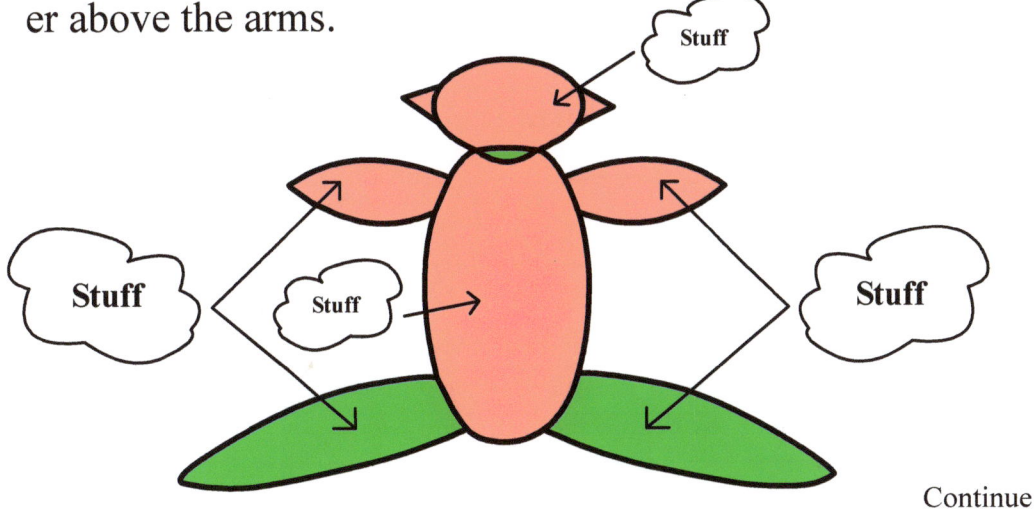

Continue...

TerryGami Gnome Instructions

10. Shape the ears in a pointed shape, tucking the excess material from the ears into the head. Sew the sides of the head and body closed. Sew the top of the shoulders together. Sew the arms. Fold the legs over 3 1/2 inches and sew the seam closed.

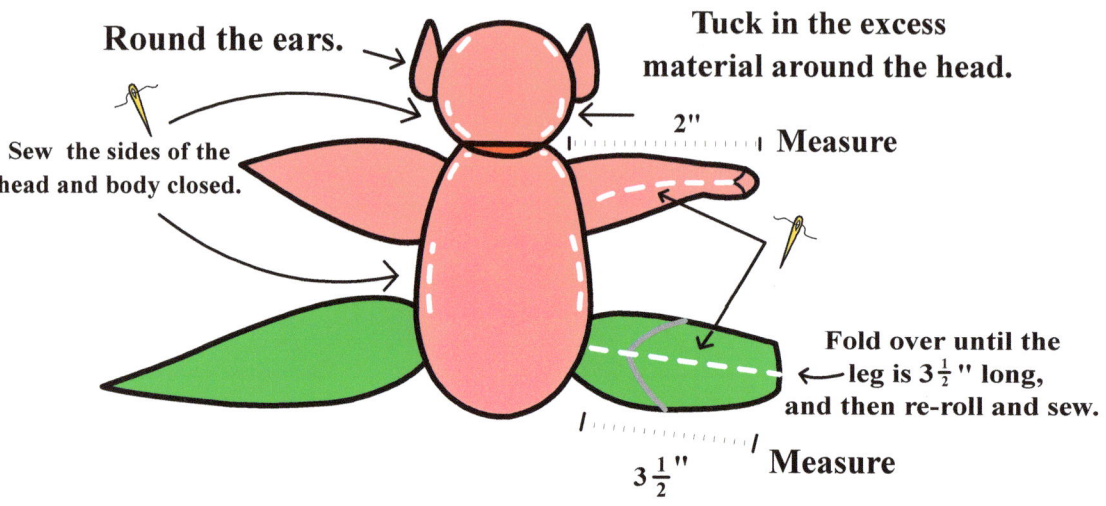

11. **To make the hands:** With the seams of the arm facing down, form a thumb so that when the palm of the hand is facing toward the back of the body, the thumb is pointing toward the body. Sew the thumb in place to form a mitten shape.

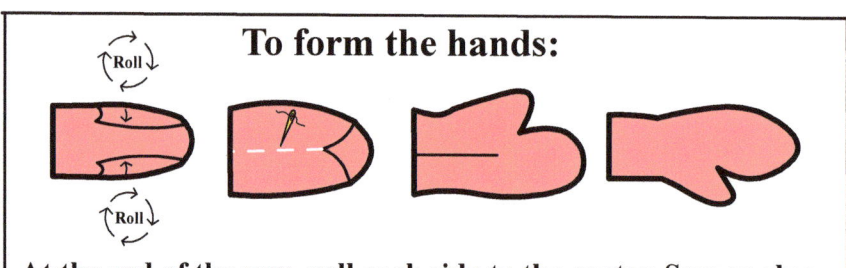

To form the hands:

At the end of the arm, roll each side to the center. Sew or glue the seams closed. Form a thumb, and then sew or glue in place. Make sure the thumb faces the body.

Continue...

TerryGami Gnome Instructions

12. Sew the legs into standing position. The boots will be the feet.

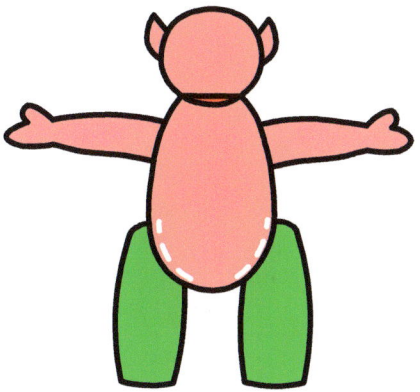

13. Note: Adjustments to the pattern may be necessary, depending on the size of the Gnome. Fold the turquise washcloth in half, place the pattern on the fold, and then cut out the pattern, but only cutting a slit at the neck on the fold side. Make sure the arm length is long enough to hem.

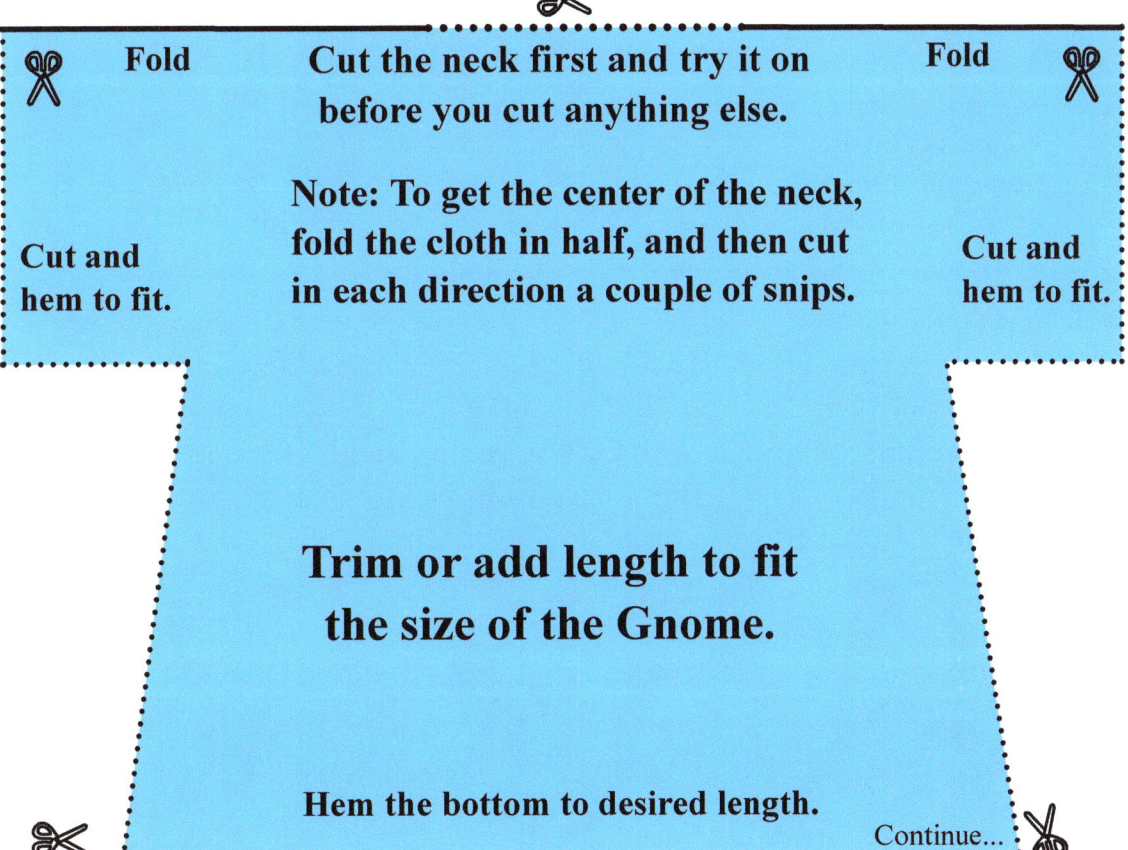

Fold

Cut the neck first and try it on before you cut anything else.

Fold

Note: To get the center of the neck, fold the cloth in half, and then cut in each direction a couple of snips.

Cut and hem to fit.

Cut and hem to fit.

Trim or add length to fit the size of the Gnome.

Hem the bottom to desired length.

Continue...

TerryGami Gnome Instructions

14. **To make the boots:** Trace the book patterns, cut them out, and then pin to the felt and cut two of each. Measure it against the Gnome's leg to make sure it won't be too wide.

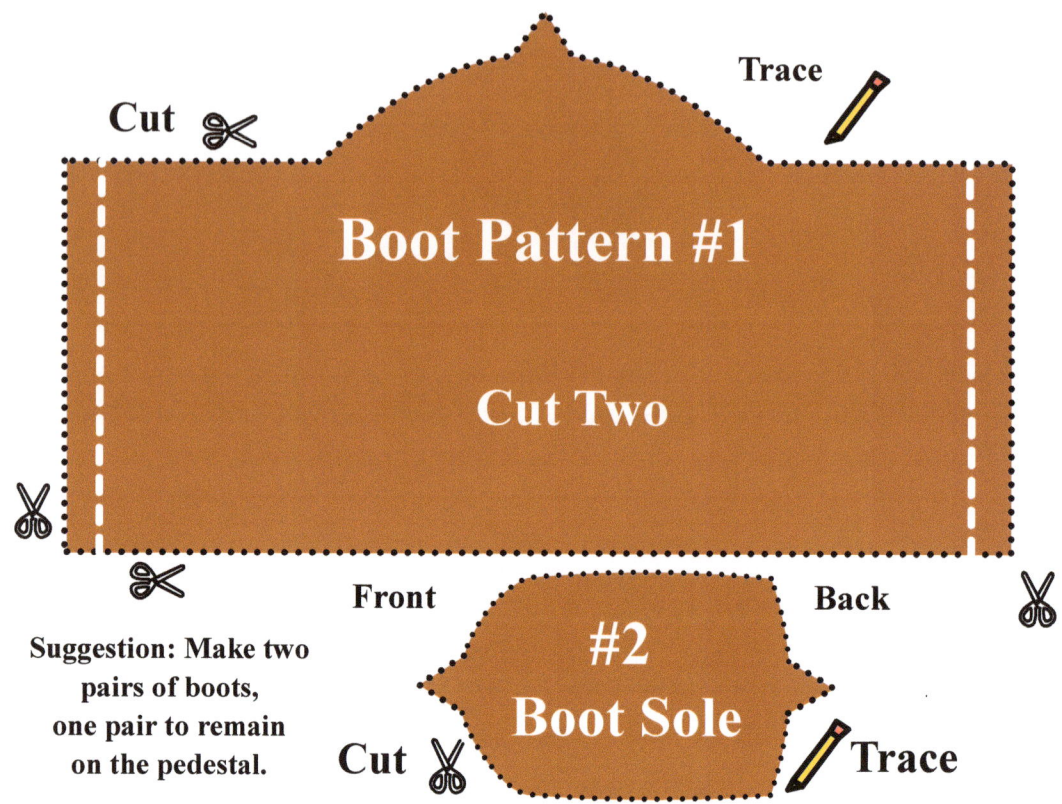

Suggestion: Make two pairs of boots, one pair to remain on the pedestal.

15. **A)** Fold the boot pattern #1 in half, and then sew up the seam leaving a 1/4-inch seam allowance. **B)** Open up the boot, and sew on the #2 boot sole, matching the arrow on the front of the boot. Line up the arrow on the back of the sole with the seam at the back of the boot. Sew the sole onto the boot. **C)** Turn it inside out. Folder over the over top of the boot to form a cuff. Pin together, if necessary.

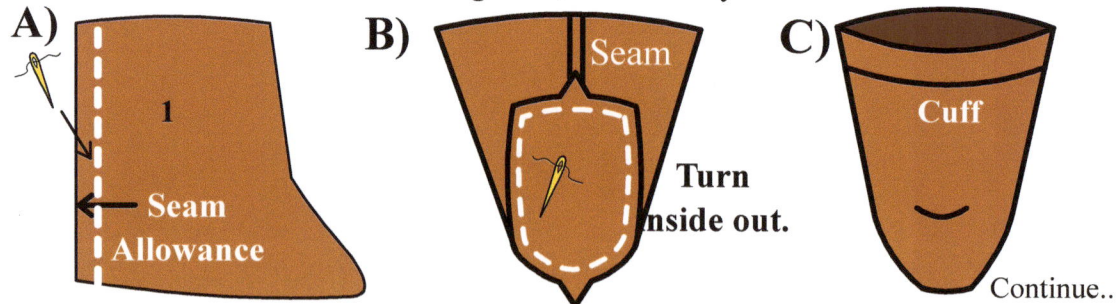

Continue...

TerryGami Gnome Instructions

16. Cut out the eyebrows, mustache and beard. Glue on the beard and mustache. Save the eyebrows for later when it is time to glue on the facial features. Cut two beard pieces so the hair and beard look full.

Eyebrows

Trace

Mustache

Trace

Beard and Hair Pattern
Cut Two

Note: Measure the pattern to the head to see if it needs to be enlarged or reduced to fit your gnome's head before you cut.

Trace

Open

Place the hole over the face.

Use quilt batting.

Trace

Continue...

TerryGami Gnome Instructions

17. **A)** Trace the pattern for the hat. Fold the material and pin on the pattern, Cut out the pattern. Wrap the material around the head to make sure it fits, and then trim the ends to fit the head, leaving a 1/4-inch seam allowance. Sew a 1/4-inch hem in the bottom of the hat, if not using felt.

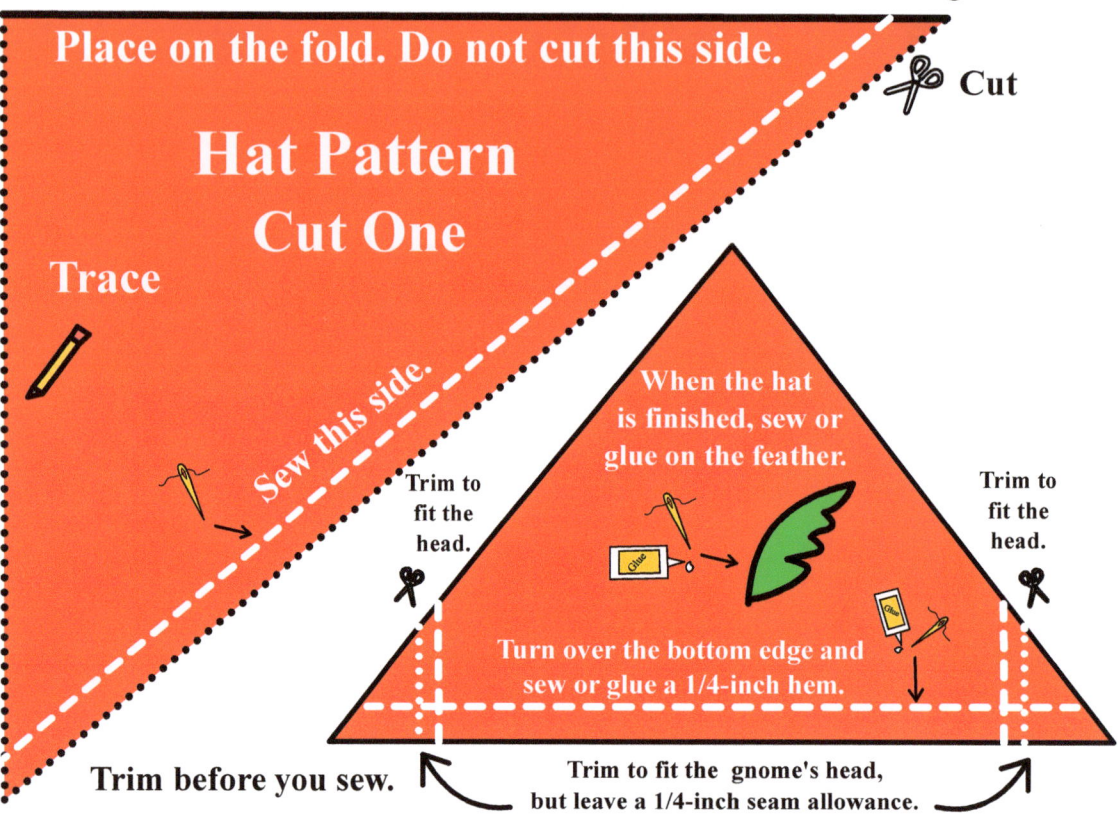

18. Fold the hat with the finished hem facing out, and then sew the edges, with a 1/4-inch seam. Turn the hat inside out. Poke the point of the hat with a pencil or pen to fully extend it.

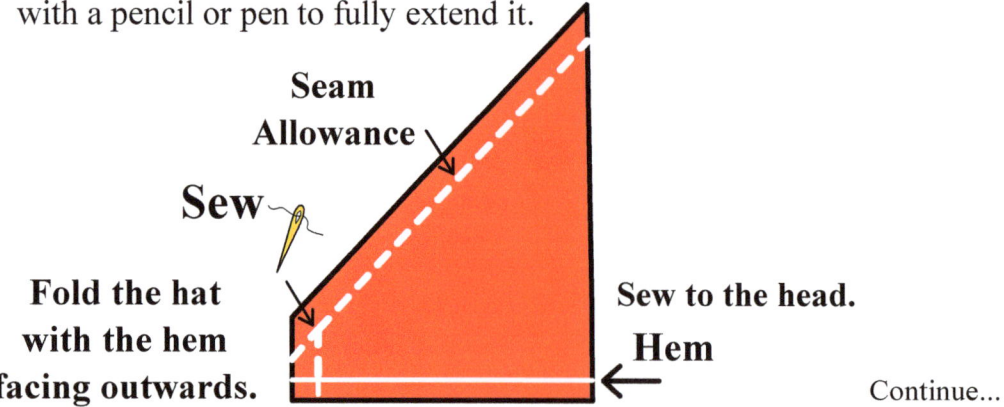

Continue...

TerryGami Gnome Instructions

19. **To Form the Pedestal:** **A)** With the second green cloth, fold the cloth in half, and then **B)** fold it in half again to form a square. **C)** Hold a string tightly at the folded corner, and with a pen or marking chalk make an arch, excluding the serged washcloth edges. **D)** Cut through all of the layers to make a circle. It does not need to be a perfect circle.

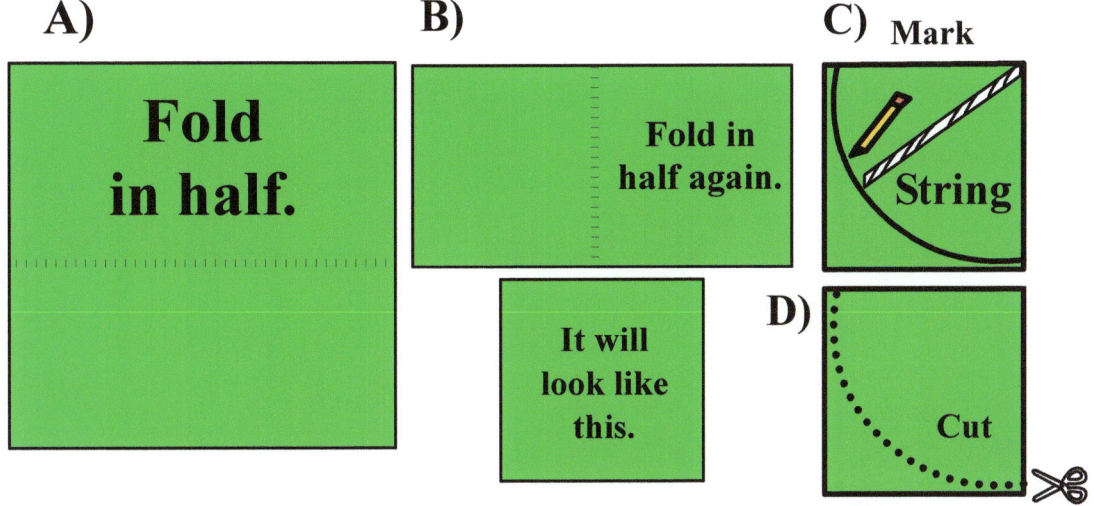

20. **A)** Use the cloth circle as a pattern to cut a piece of quilt batting. Place it on top of the washcloth circle. Sew a running stitch 1/4 inch from the edge around the entire circle. Add the pebbles to the center and **B)** begin to pull the thread tightly so it will gather the material all of the way together to form the bottom of the pedestal. Fill with more pebbles, if necessary. Sew the bottom closed, and turn it over.

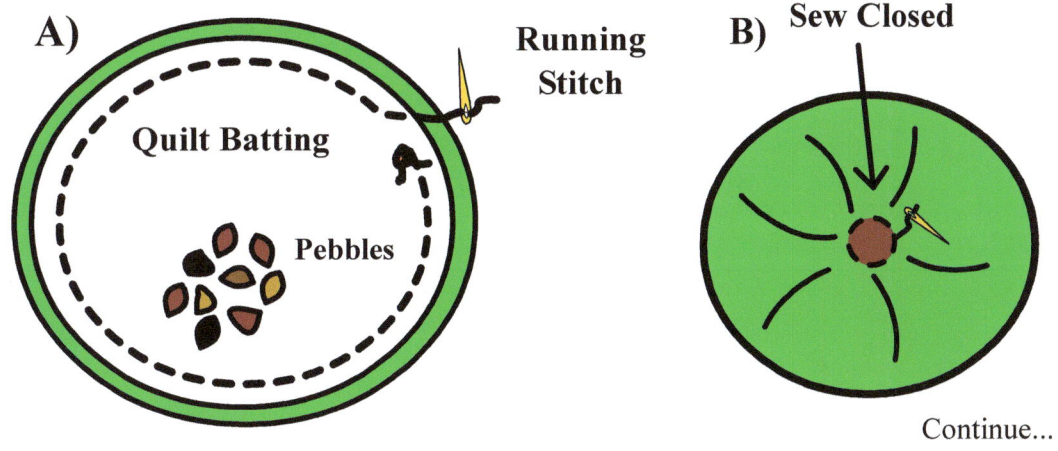

Continue...

21. TerryGami Gnome Instructions

Trace patterns and prepare the facial features from foam board or felt. Attach the quilt batting beard, eye brows and mustache. Use hole punch for the eyes, nose, mouth and cheeks. Make the patterns for the belt and belt buckle, and cut out. Sew or glue on the belt and belt buckle. Sew or glue on the feather to the hat. Sew or glue the flowers to one hand and the walkng stick to the other. Attach the Velcro strips to the boots and to the pedestal. Place the gnome in the boots. Place the chop stick or stick up the back of the shirt and hat. Use it and the walking stick to help balance the gnome on his feet. Trim any snags in the material.

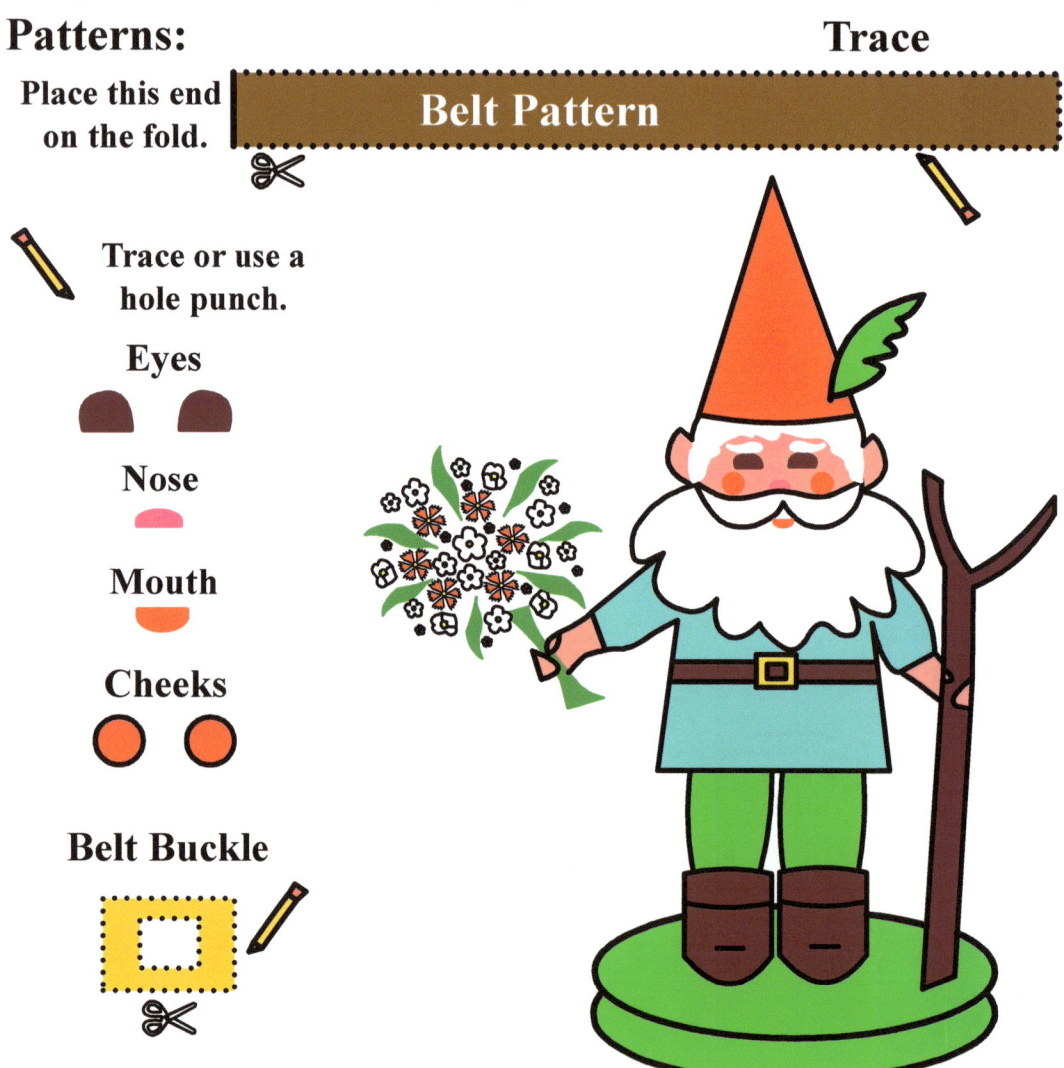

Patterns:

Place this end on the fold.

Belt Pattern

Trace

Trace or use a hole punch.

Eyes

Nose

Mouth

Cheeks

Belt Buckle

Warning: Keep sharp objects, small materials and rubber bands away from babies and small children.

Gnome Factoids

- Female gnomes adorn themselves with flowers and berries.
- Gnomes kiss by rubbing noses.
- Gnomes are said to live underground and are be able to move through the earth as easily as we move through the air.
- Garden gnomes became popular in the 19th century.
- Gnomes are said to be very kind and caring, and, if you deserve it, they will lend you a helping hand.

TerryGami Gnome Girl Instructions

Materials
* Two thin, white terrycloth washcloths approximately 12" x 12"
* One thin, peach terrycloth washcloth approximately 12" x 12"
* One thin, pink terrycloth washcloth apprximately 12" x 12" for the clothes
* One thin, green terrycloth washcloth approximately 12" x 12" for the pedestal
* Six pipe cleaners (optional for legs)
* Clear fabric glue (non-toxic and non-flammable)
* Chop stick or 12" stick, if making a standing Gnome
* Ten pieces of brown yarn 24" long pieces, four 4-inch strands
* Small pieces of brown, red, peach foam board or felt for eyes, nose and cheeks
* Needle and matching thread
* Brown felt square for boots
* Pink yarn or ribbon for hair bows
* Red tatting thread or yarn for mouth 1 1/2"
* Three medium rubber bands
* Tiny basket with berries (optional)
* Quilt batting
* Hole punch 1/4"
* Scissors
* Ruler

Note: It is better to sew this doll, rather than glue it. Allow a lot of time for this project!

Finished size: Approximately 7"w x 12" h.

1. Cut the tags off of all of the cloths. Place each of the two white cloths flat on a flat surface in a diamond shape. Roll the top and bottom corners to the center of each cloth. If making a Gnome standing on a pedestal (See step #17), roll the pipe cleaners into the cloth for the legs. Trim the ends of the pipe cleaners to fit or bend the ends over.

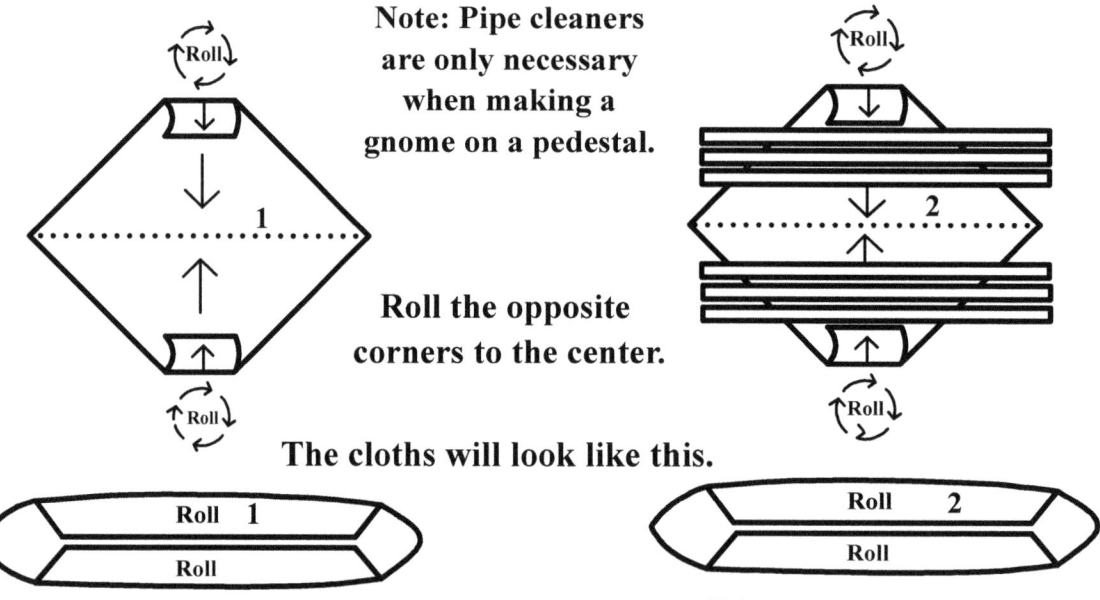

Note: Pipe cleaners are only necessary when making a gnome on a pedestal.

Roll the opposite corners to the center.

The cloths will look like this.

This cloth will be half of the body.   This cloth will be the legs.

Continue...

TerryGami Gnome Girl Instructions

2. **A)** Place the third cloth on a flat surface in a diamond shape. **B)** Fold the top and bottom corners so that the corners meet in the center. **C)** Turn the cloth over, holding the corners in place. Pin or lightly tape in place, if necessary. **D)** Roll the folded sides to the center. The corners will flip up. **E)** The cloth will look like this. This cloth will be part of the body. The center corners will become the ears. Turn the cloth over so it doesn't unroll.

A)

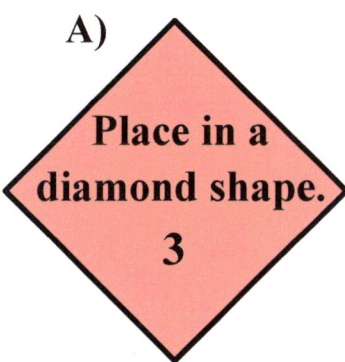

B) Fold the top and bottom corners to meet in the center.

C) Flip over with corners in place.

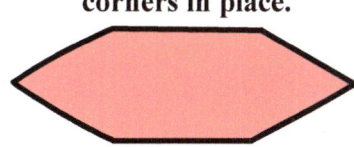

D) Roll the sides to the center.

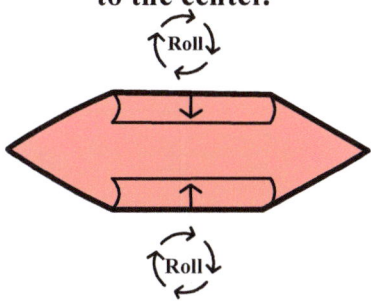

E) This is what the cloth will look like.

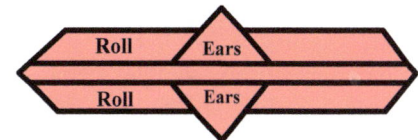

This piece is part of the body.

Continue...

TerryGami Gnome Girl Instructions

3. Stack cloth one (the body cloth) and cloth three (the ear cloth). Cloth number three should be on the bottom with the rolls facing down, and cloth number one should be on top with the rolls facing up.

Stack the cloths.

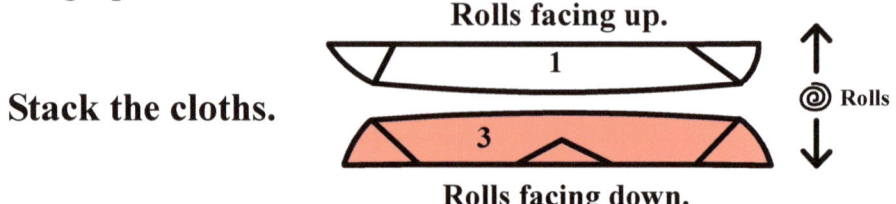

---

4. Measure down 5 inches from the corners on each end, and then wrap rubber bands.

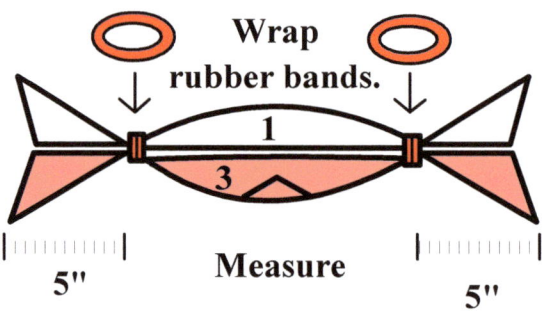

---

5. Now turn the ensemble inside out so that all of the corners are on the inside, including the corners that will become the ears. The rolls will be on the inside.

Turn the ensemble inside out.   **The corners will actually fill the entire hole.**

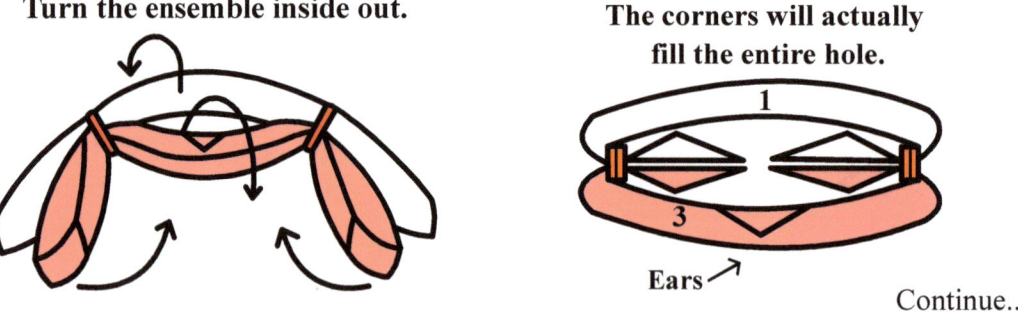

Continue...

TerryGami Gnome Girl Instructions

6. Pull the corners out, one on each side, top and bottom. Turn the cloth upright with the peach cloth on the right side. **Note:** The top and bottom corners will be switched later so that the arms and skirt colors will match. There will be peach arms and a white skirt.

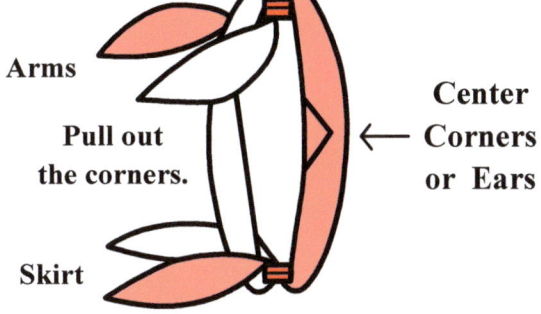

Arms
Pull out the corners.
Skirt
Center Corners or Ears

7. **To form the head: A)** Roll the peach side up. Make sure the "ears" or center corners are above the rubber band. **B)** Measure down 2 inches from the top. Wrap a rubber band at this point.

Side View

A) Roll upward.
← Center Corners or Ears
Roll this side of the cloth upwards.

B) 2"
← Back of head
Wrap a rubber band.
Important! This is the front of the body.

Continue...

TerryGami Gnome Girl Instructions

8. To form the legs: Pull white leg cloth (number 2) through the bottom part of the body with the rolls facing down. Make sure the legs are even. Separate the rolls slightly inside of the head and stomach, and then stuff in between rolls. Note: The body may not need stuffing.

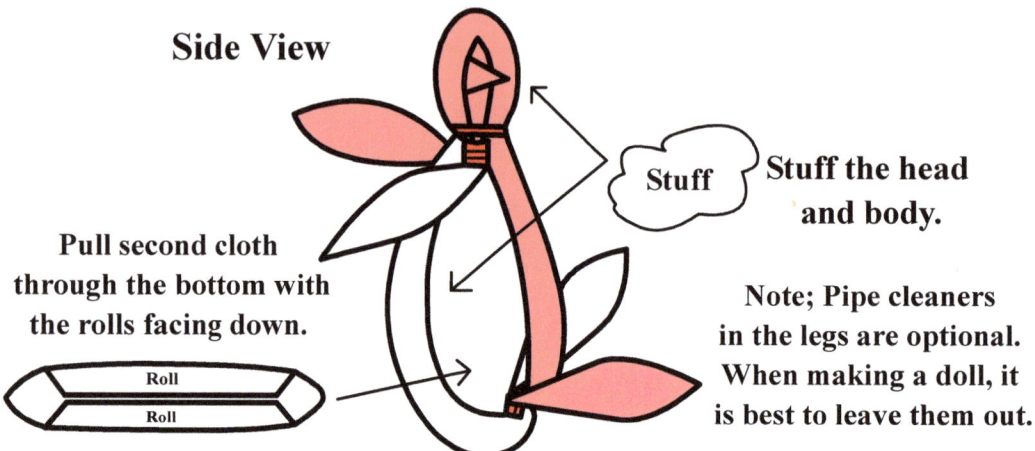

9. On the side with the peach corner on the bottom, rearrange the corners so the peach corner is on the top to match the other arm. The white corners on the bottom will be the skirt of the apron. For the ears: Tuck in the excess material and adjust the ears upward and into a point.

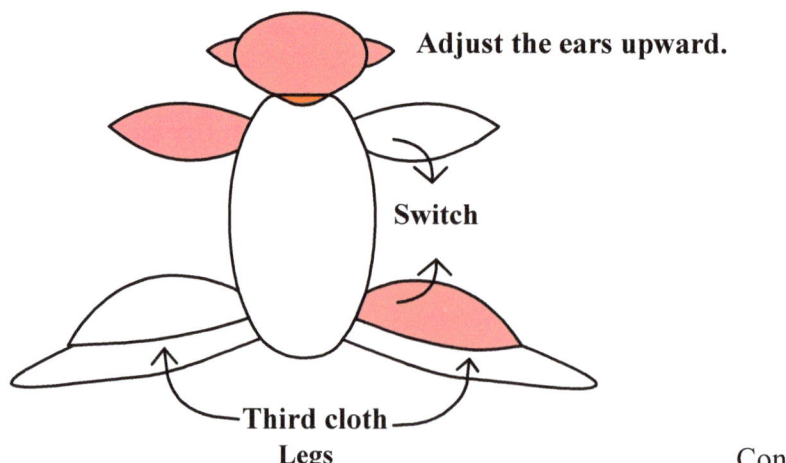

Continue...

TerryGami Gnome Girl Instructions

10. **For the arms and legs: A)** Twist the seams of the arms and legs in a downward position, and then re-roll them. Stuff them with strips of quilt batting. **B)** Sew or glue the seams closed on each, making sure to form wrists on the arms and to make ankles on the legs. **Note:** See the next page for two options for making the hands and feet. Sew or glue the sides of the head, shoulders and body.

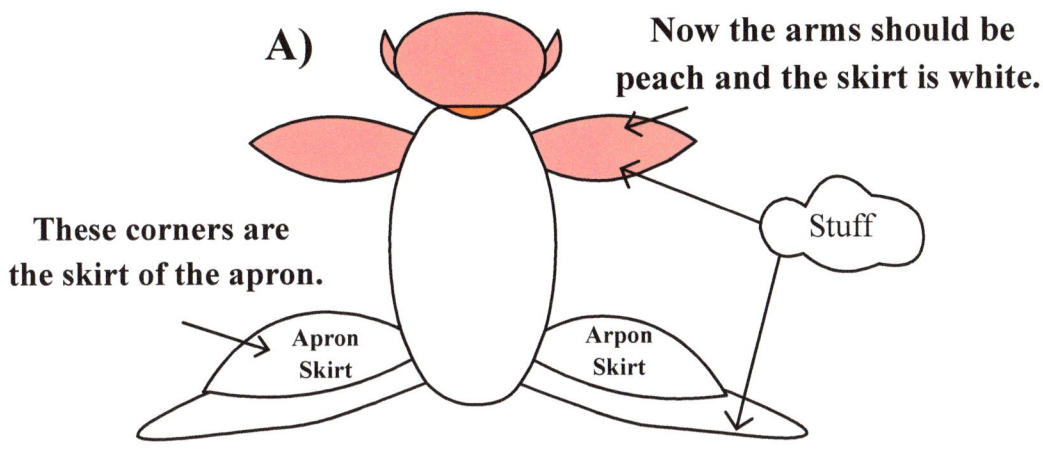

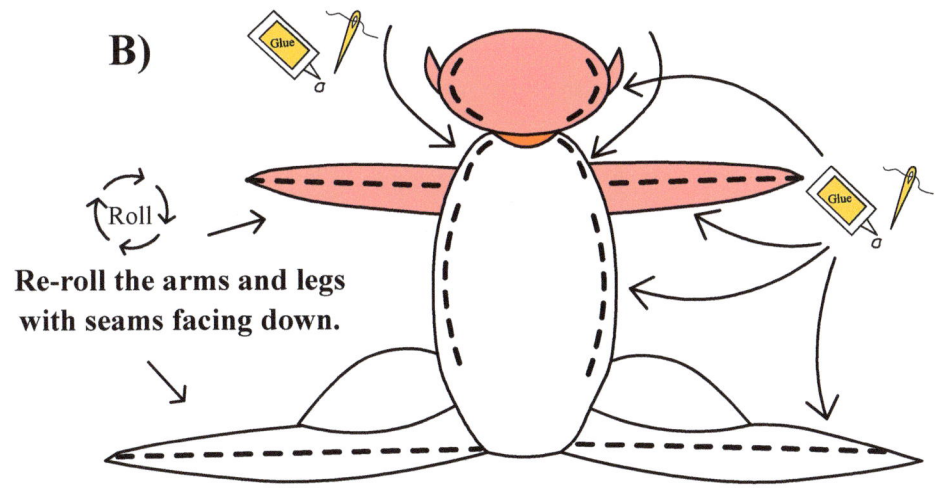

Continue...

11. TerryGami Gnome Girl Instructions

There are two choices for both the hands and the feet in the boxes below. For the hands, choose the box below depending on how detailed you want to make them. Make sure the thumbs face the body when the palms are facing the back of the body. For a standing gnome, box A is better for the "feet" because it provides sturdier legs. The boots will make the feet. For a gnome without the pedestal, use box B for the feet. Make boots for both options.

For the gnome standing on a pedestal, the boots will be the feet.

Hands

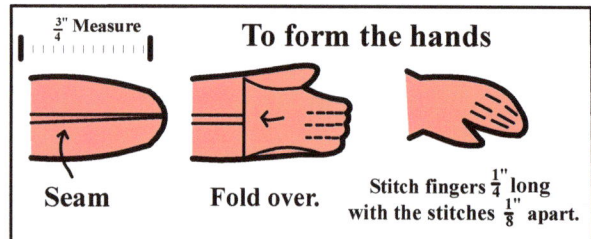

To form the hands

Seam. Fold over. Stitch fingers $\frac{1}{4}$" long with the stitches $\frac{1}{8}$" apart.

$\frac{3}{4}$" Measure

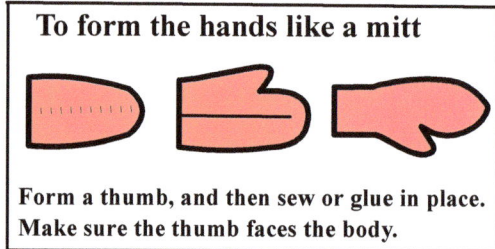

To form the hands like a mitt

Form a thumb, and then sew or glue in place. Make sure the thumb faces the body.

Feet

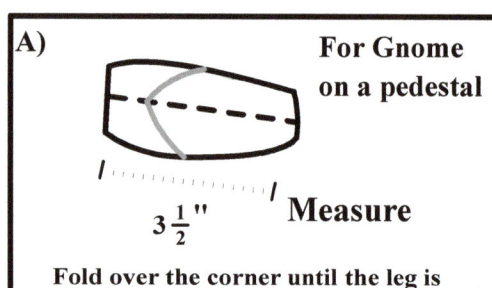

A) For Gnome on a pedestal

$3\frac{1}{2}$" Measure

Fold over the corner until the leg is 3 1/2" long, and then re-roll and sew. Be sure to bend the pipe cleaners.

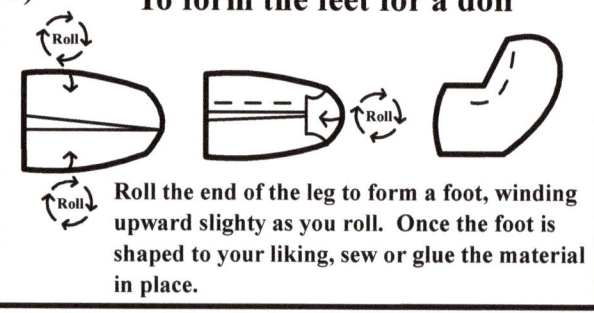

B) To form the feet for a doll

Roll the end of the leg to form a foot, winding upward slighty as you roll. Once the foot is shaped to your liking, sew or glue the material in place.

Continue...

TerryGami Gnome Girl Instructions

12. Unravel the skirt corners, and then pull them together in front at the waist. Join the corners and sew or glue them to form the skirt of the apron, leaving a upside-down little "V" at the bottom.

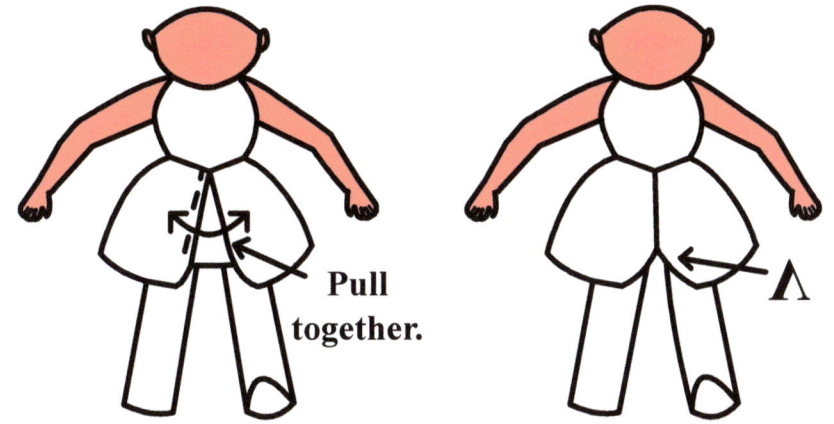

13. **To make the bell-shaped sleeves:** From one of the pink cloths, measure down 1 1/2 inches from the corner on two of the corners, and then cut the corners off. Fold over the rough edges 1/4 inch as you work. Wrap the corner aound the arm pits with the seams under the arms, and then trim the material to fit, leaving a 1/4-inch seam allowance. Sew the seams together under the arms and sew the sleeve to the doll. Cut the 1-inch corners off of the washcloth for the collar on the next page.

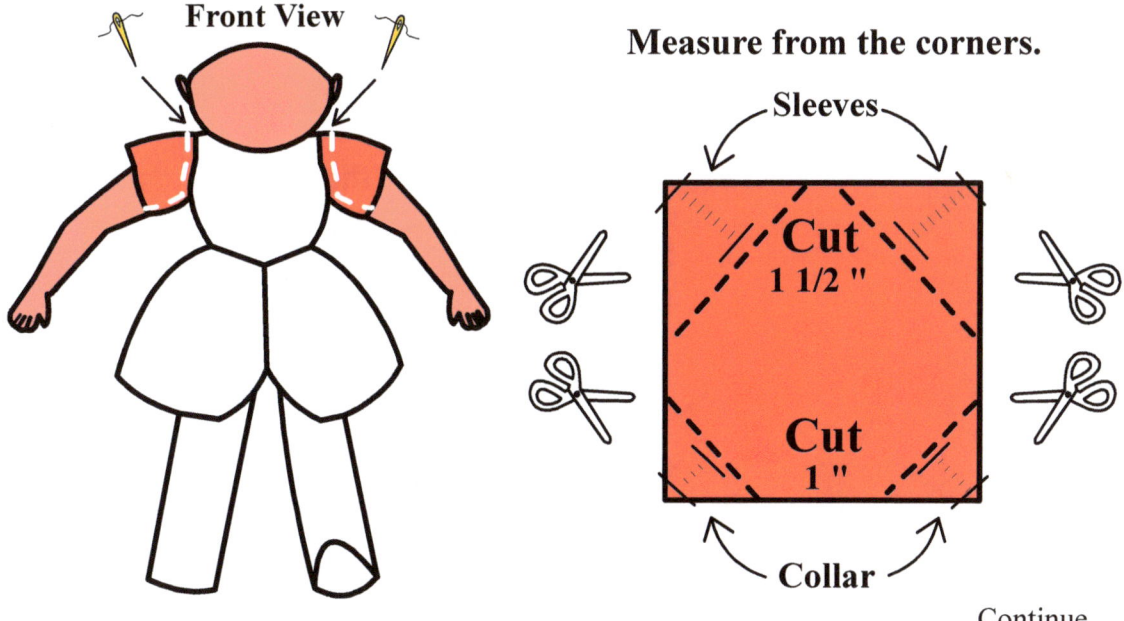

Continue...

TerryGami Gnome Girl Instructions

14. **To make the collar:** Cut the remaining 1 inch corners from the pink washcloth (on the previous page). Fold one end over, and then fit the collar to the doll. Trim off the excess material on that one side, leaving a 1/4-inch seam allowance so the rough edges of the collar can be turned under and sew down. Repeat with the other corner. Sew the collar together in the front. With the remaining excess material on each corner, make a "V" in the back of the doll (see step #15).

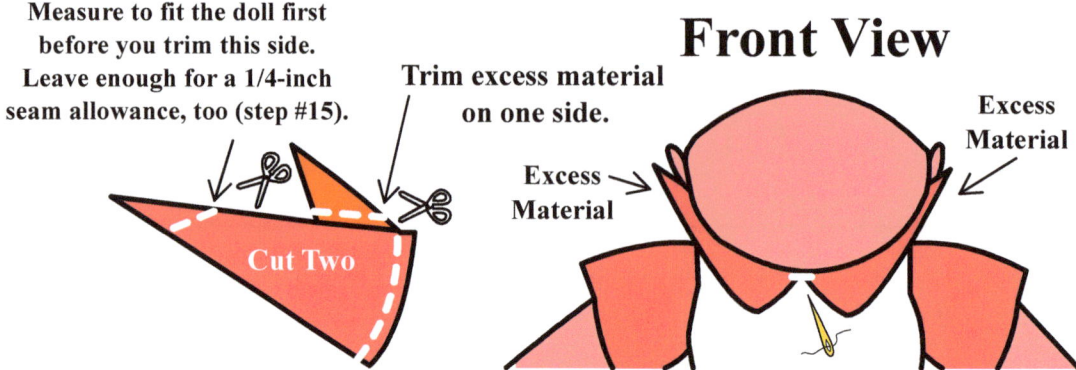

15. With the remaining sides of the collar pieces, drape them down the back of the doll. Cut the end piece on a slant as shown above, making a V at the waist. Later, sew the point to the skirt. Finish the back of the collar by cutting a separate 1 x 3-inch rectangle from the edge of the remaining pink cloth. Fold over the the rough edge of the rectangle, sew down the seam, and then sew the rectangle to the inside of the straps.

Cut a rectangle to finish the back of the collar.

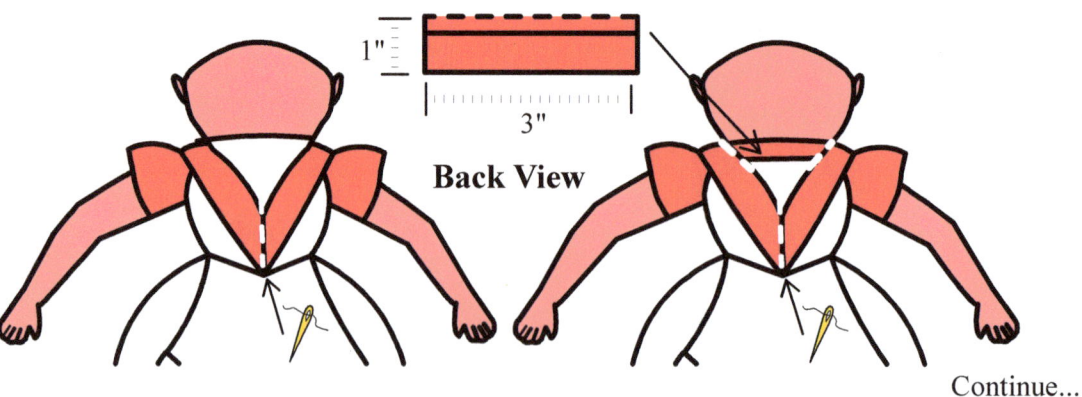

Continue...

TerryGami Gnome Girl Instructions

16. **To make the skirt: A)** Measure 3 1/4 inches from one edge of a pink washcloth. (Note: You may want to measure against the Gnome to determine the length of the skirt.) Mark and cut the cloth across the entire length of the washcloth. **B)** Fold over the rough edge 1/4 inch, and sew a running stitch to tack down the edge (see the Sewing by Hand page). **C)** When you reach the end, instead of tying off the thread, pull the thread to gather the material first to fit the Gnome's waist. Now tie off the thread. **D)** Sew the seam of the skirt closed. Put the skirt on the doll and sew the skirt to the collar at the point in the back. Drape the apron over the skirt in the front.

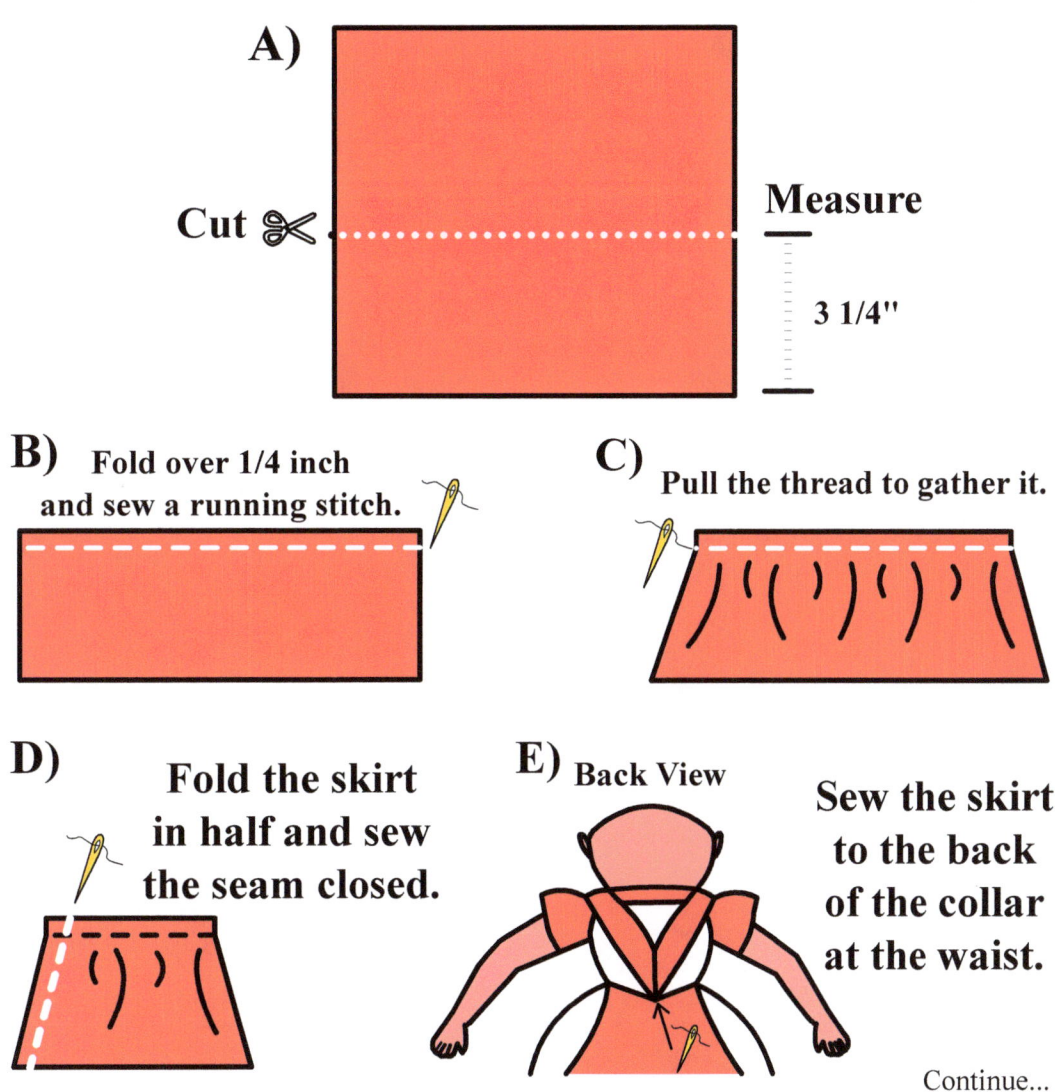

A) Cut — Measure 3 1/4"

B) Fold over 1/4 inch and sew a running stitch.

C) Pull the thread to gather it.

D) Fold the skirt in half and sew the seam closed.

E) Back View — Sew the skirt to the back of the collar at the waist.

Continue...

17. TerryGami Gnome Girl Instructions

A) Divide the 20 strands of brown yarn in half, leaving 10 strands each. Fold each group of ten strands in half, and then **B)** measure down 1 inch from the fold on each grouping. Gather the yarn together at this point. **C)** Sew the hair to the head at the gather point. **D)** Braid each side and tie off with a bow of pink yarn. **E)** Cut four 4-inch strands, fold them in half, and then **F)** sew or glue them above the ear.

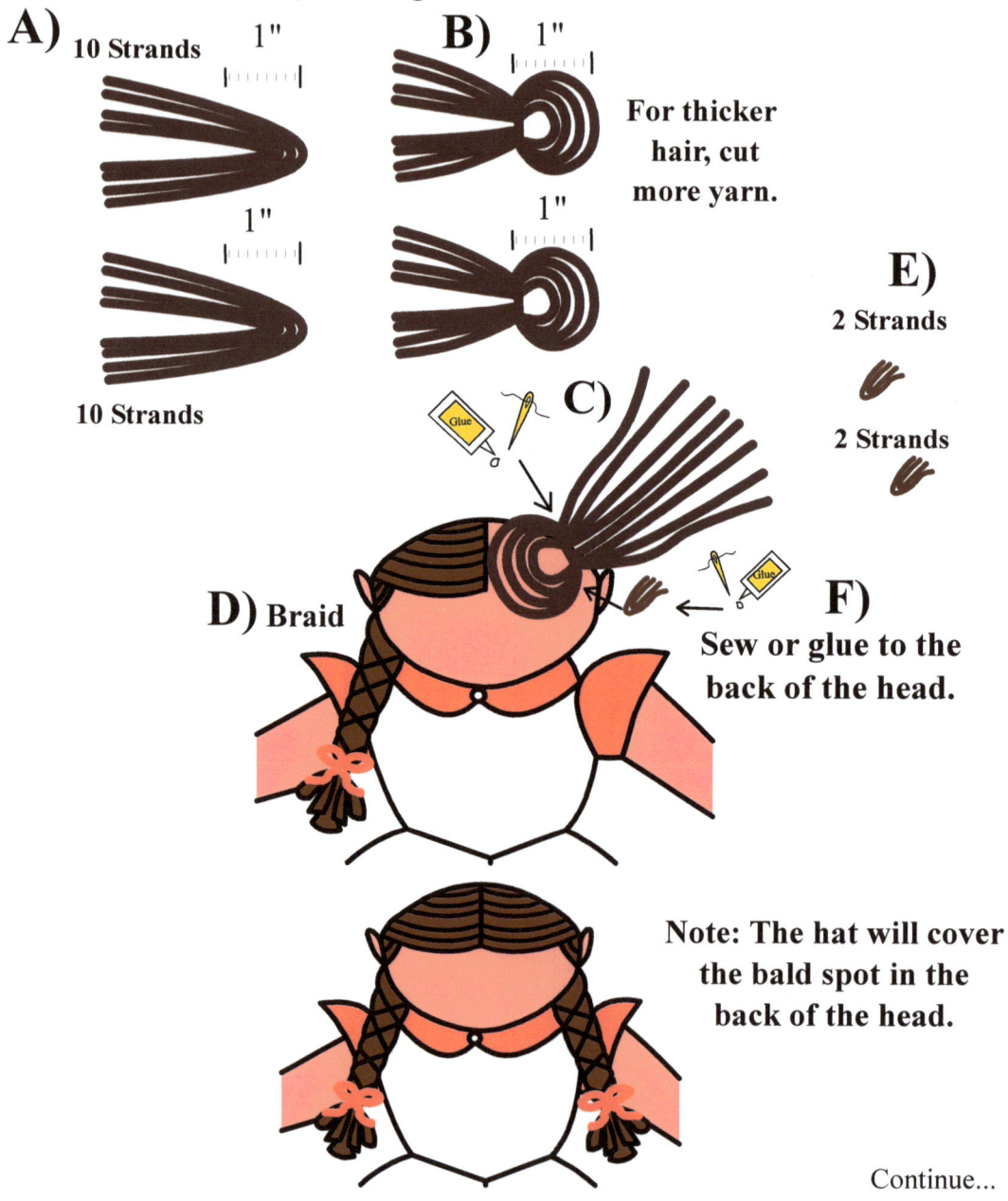

For thicker hair, cut more yarn.

Note: The hat will cover the bald spot in the back of the head.

Continue...

TerryGami Gnome Girl Instructions

18. **A)** Trace the pattern for the hat. Fold the material and pin on the pattern, Cut the material, making sure not to cut the fold side. Wrap the material around the head to make sure the hat fits, and then trim the ends to fit the head, leaving a 1/4-inch seam allowance. Sew a 1/4-inch hem in the bottom of the hat, if using terrycloth. There is no need for a hem if you are using felt.

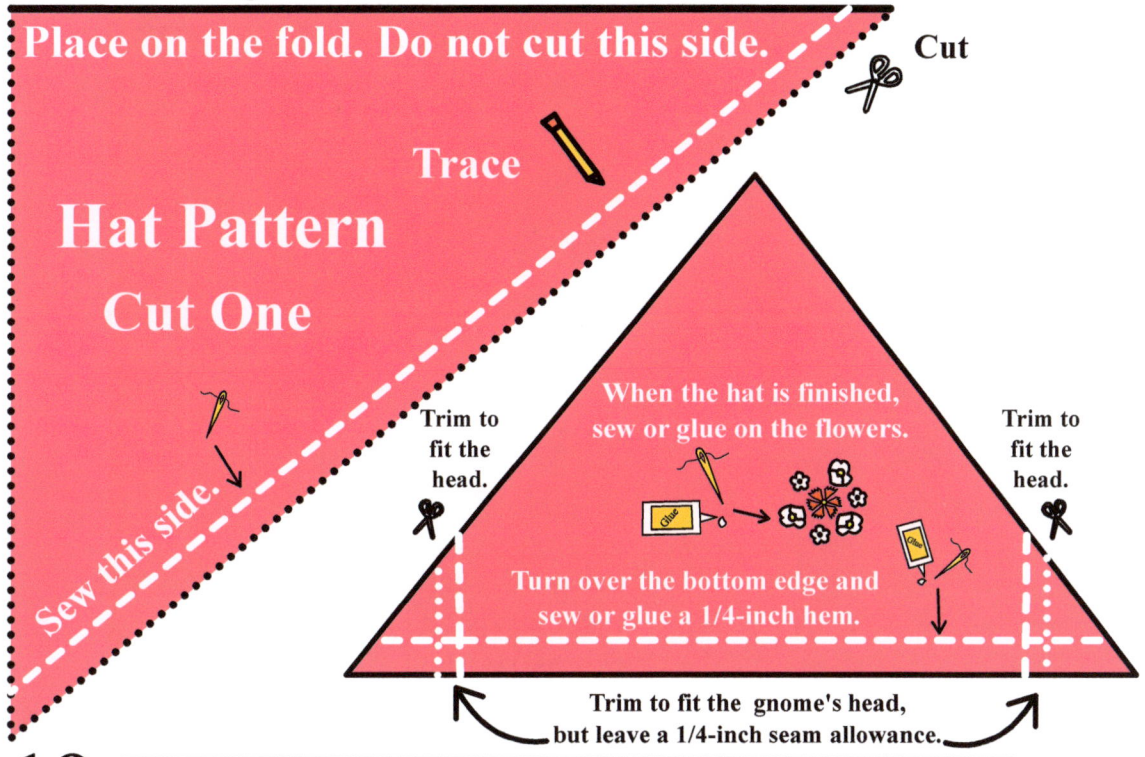

19. Fold the hat with the finished hem facing out, and then sew the edges, with a 1/4-inch seam. Turn the hat inside out. Poke the point of the hat with a pencil or pen to fully extend it. Sew it to the head.

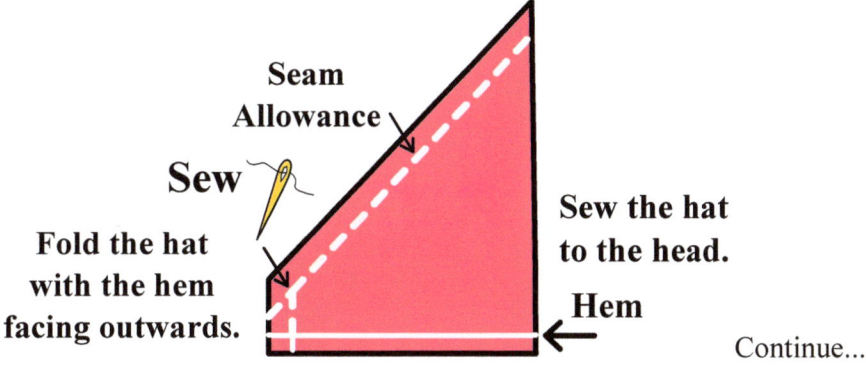

Continue...

TerryGami Gnome Girl Instructions

20. **To make the boots:** Trace the book patterns, cut them out, and then pin to the felt and cut two of each. Measure it against the Gnome's leg to make sure it won't be too wide.

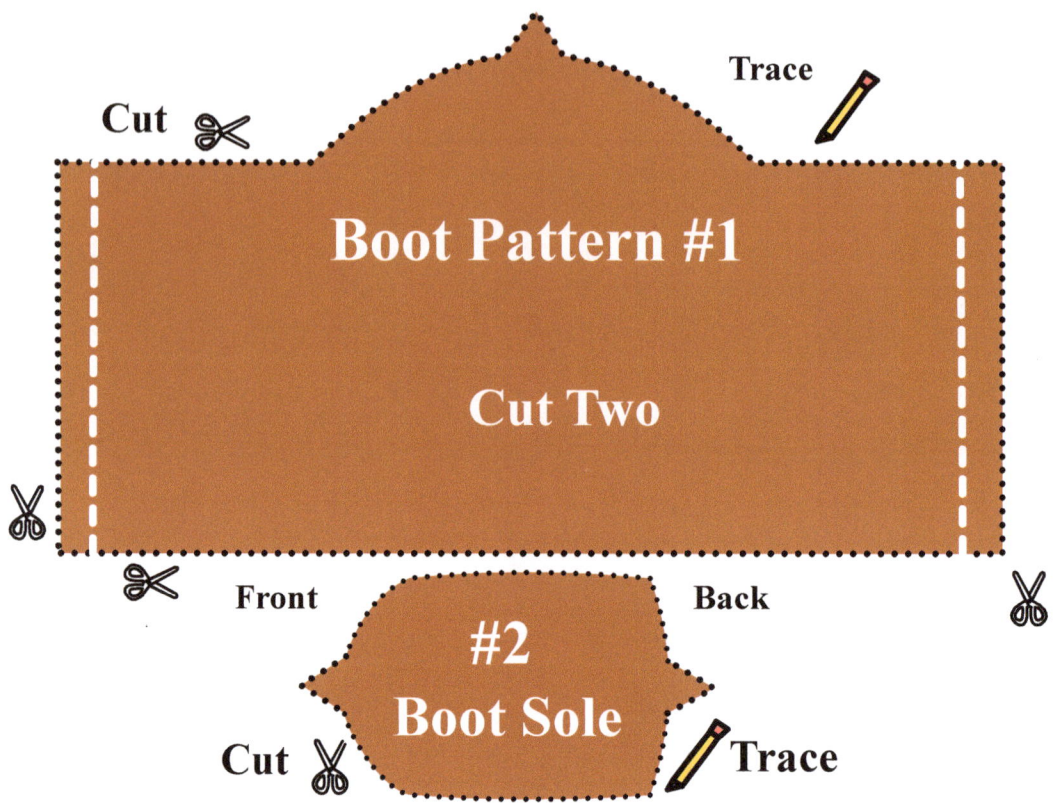

21. **A)** Fold the boot pattern #1 in half, and then sew up the seam leaving a 1/4-inch seam allowance. **B)** Open up the boot, and sew on the #2 boot sole, matching the arrow on the front of the boot. Line up the arrow on the back of the sole with the seam at the back of the boot. Sew the sole onto the boot. C) Turn it inside out. Folder over the over top of the boot to form a cuff. Pin together, if necessary.

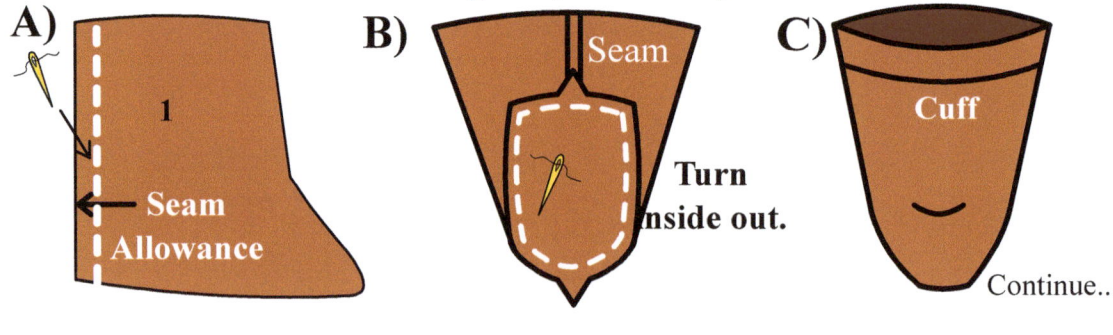

Continue...

TerryGami Gnome Girl Instructions

22. **To Form the Pedestal:** **A)** With the second green cloth, fold the cloth in half, and then **B)** fold it in half again to form a square. **C)** Hold a string tightly at the folded corner, and with a pen or marking chalk make an arch, excluding the serged washcloth edges. **D)** Cut through all of the layers to make a circle. It does not need to be a perfect circle.

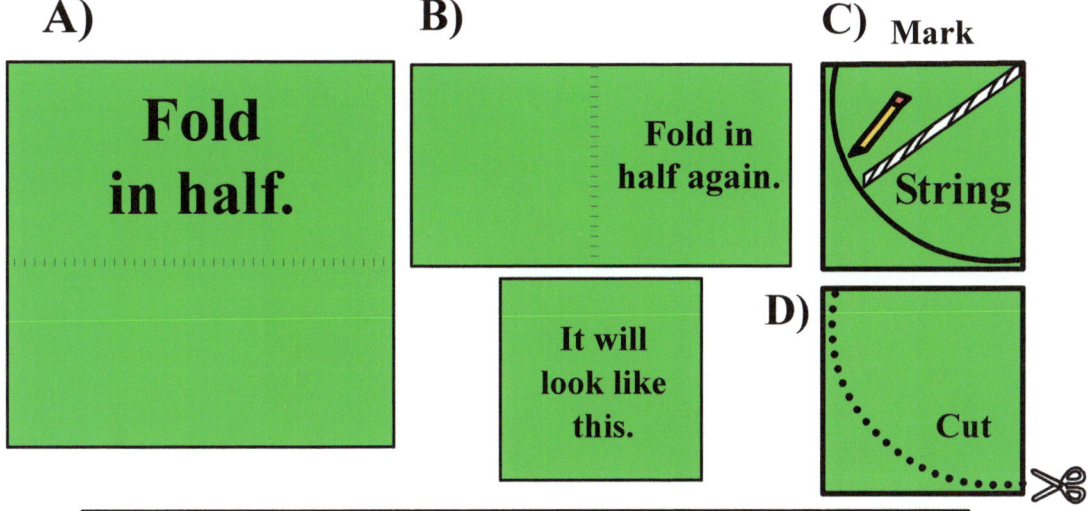

23. **A)** Use the cloth circle as a pattern to cut a piece of quilt batting. Place it on top of the washcloth circle. Sew a running stitch 1/4 inch from the edge around the entire circle. Add the pebbles to the center and **B)** begin to pull the thread tightly so it will gather the material all of the way together to form the bottom of the pedestal. Fill with more pebbles, if necessary. Sew the bottom closed, and turn it over.

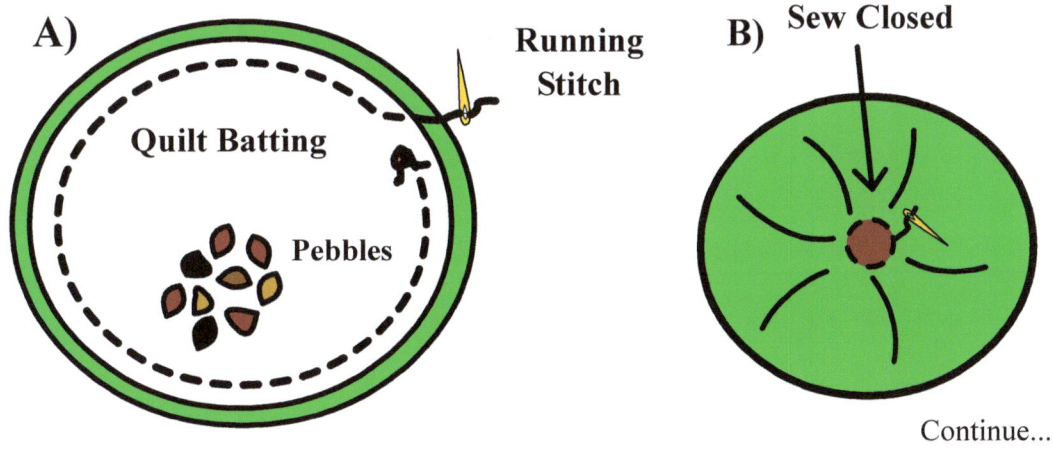

Continue...

24. TerryGami Gnome Girl Instructions

Trace and cut out the eyes, cheeks and nose or use a hole punch. Cut about a 1/2-inch piece of yarn or tatting thread for the mouth. Glue on the facial features. Glue on a heart to the front of the apron. Sew the walking stick and the basket to the hands. Attach the Velcro® strips to the boots and to the pedestal. Place the gnome in the boots. Place the stick through the back of the shirt and hat. Use a chop stick or a stick and the walking stick to help balance the gnome on his feet. Trim any snags in the material. Note: Cover the stick with brown felt (optional).

Patterns:

✂ Cut   ✏ Trace or use hole punch.

Heart

Eyes

Nose

Cheeks

1"

Mouth
Trim to fit the gnome.

Make two pairs of boots, one pair to remain on the pedestal.

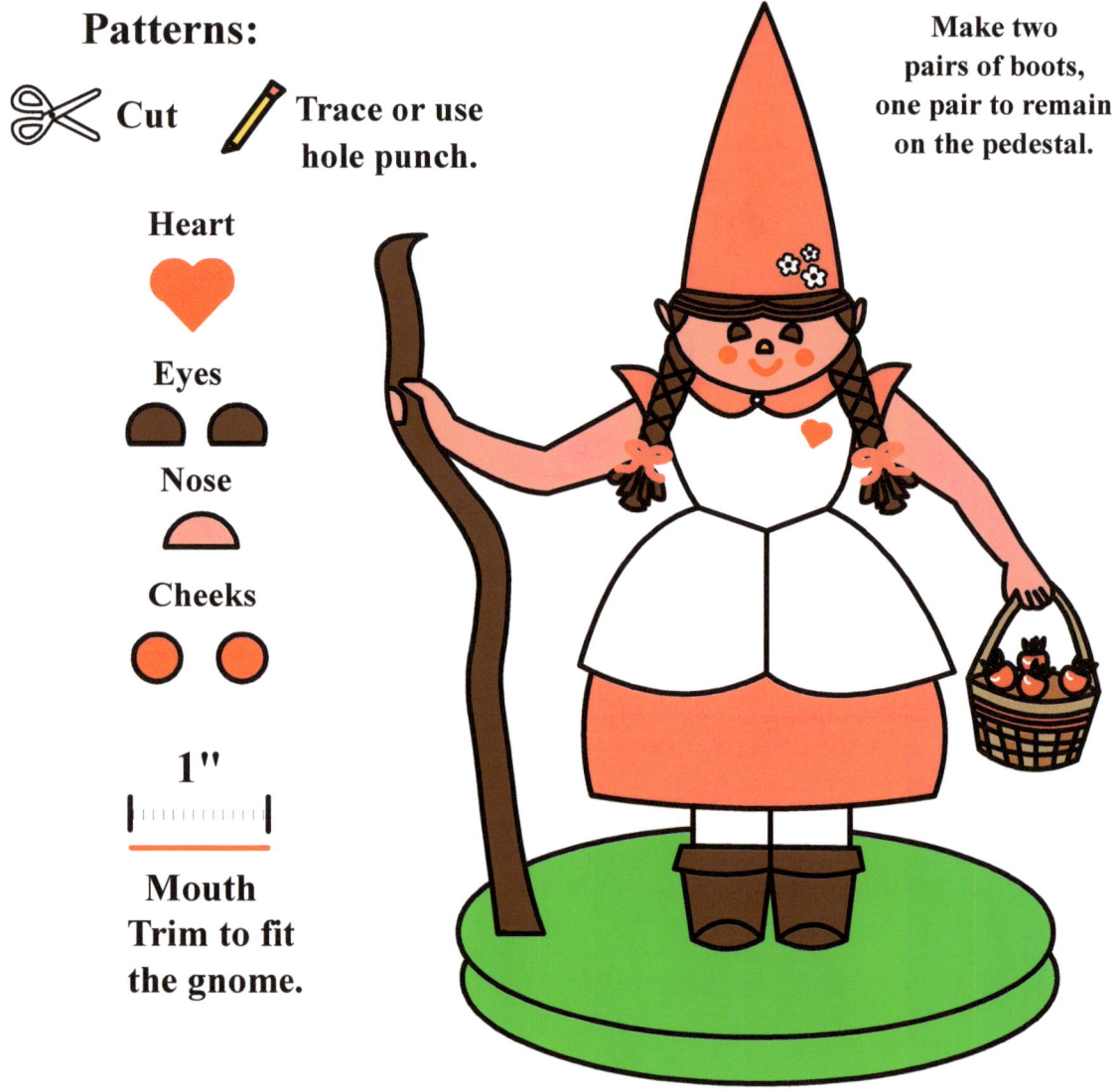

Warning: Keep sharp objects, small materials and rubber bands away from babies and small children.

TerryGami Elf Shoe Instructions

Cut two of the elf shoe pattern below. Fold each in half and sew across the bottom and up and around the toe, leaving about about an inch open at the top. Once sewn, turn the shoes inside out. Cut two yellow and black squares, glue them together with the yellow on top, and then glue on the buckles to the top of the shoes.

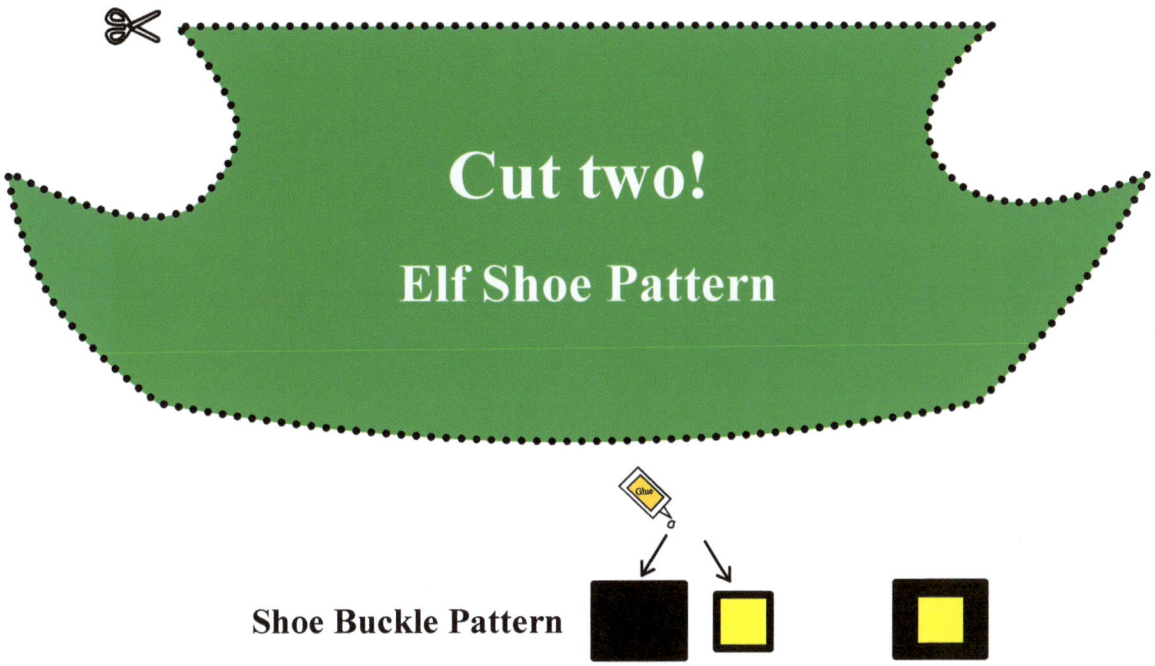

Shoe Buckle Pattern

Once sewn, turn the shoes inside out.

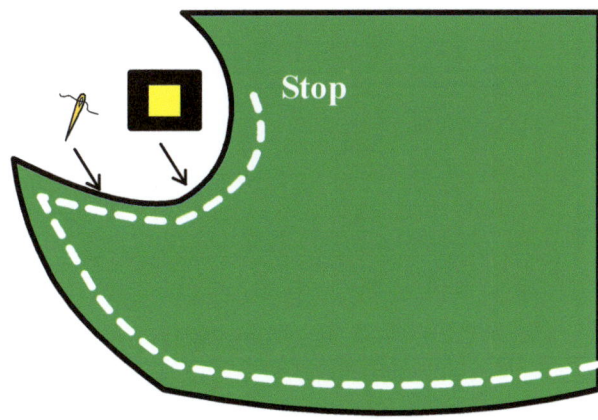

Warning: Keep sharp objects, small materials and rubber bands away from babies and small children.

www.ingramcontent.com/pod-product-compliance
Lightning Source LLC
Chambersburg PA
CBHW042022150426
43198CB00002B/44